SO-BYG-303

# THE ART OF YOUTH

# Also by Nicholas Delbanco

FICTION

*Sherbrookes*
(one volume, revised)

*The Count of Concord*

*Spring and Fall*

*The Vagabonds*

*What Remains*

*Old Scores*

*In the Name of Mercy*

*The Writers' Trade, and Other Stories*

*About My Table, and Other Stories*

*Stillness*

*Sherbrookes*

*Possession*

*Small Rain*

*Fathering*

*In the Middle Distance*

*News*

*Consider Sappho Burning*

*Grasse, 3/23/66*

*The Martlet's Tale*

# THE ART
# OF YOUTH

*Crane, Carrington, Gershwin,*
*and the Nature of First Acts*

## Nicholas Delbanco

NEW HARVEST
HOUGHTON MIFFLIN HARCOURT
BOSTON • NEW YORK
2013

This edition published by special arrangement with Amazon Publishing

For information about permission to reproduce selections from this book,
write to Permissions, Houghton Mifflin Harcourt Publishing Company,
215 Park Avenue South, New York, New York 10003.

www.hmhbooks.com

*Library of Congress Cataloging-in-Publication Data*
Delbanco, Nicholas.
The art of youth : Crane, Carrington, Gershwin, and the nature of first acts /
Nicholas Delbanco.
pages  cm
ISBN 978-0-544-11446-3 (hardback)
1. Artists—Biography. 2. Young artists. 3. Crane, Stephen, 1871–1900.
4. Carrington, Dora de Houghton, 1893–1932. 5. Gershwin, George, 1898–1937.
I. Title.
NX90.D45 2013
700.83—dc23    2013026090

Printed in the United States of America
DOC 10 9 8 7 6 5 4 3 2 1

*For Elena*

*Again, Again*

# Introduction

My candle burns at both ends;
It will not last the night;
But ah, my foes, and oh, my friends —
It gives a lovely light.

— EDNA ST. VINCENT MILLAY

SEARCHING FOR SUGAR MAN is a documentary about the singer-songwriter Sixto Rodriguez. I saw it weeks ago, and it has stayed with me since. Malik Bendjelloul's film describes the musician's career in the late 1960s and the early '70s, his disappearance from his native Detroit, and his iconic stature in South Africa. A rising star to start with, Rodriguez — also known as Sugar Man — wrote and sang in the protest mode of the young Bob Dylan. Playing guitar in smoke-filled rooms, black-garbed and lean, he turned his back on the audience, chanting. Mystery attached to him; he had physical strength, a mournful demeanor, and no fixed address. He conducted his business meetings in alleys; he slept, it would seem, on the streets. Although the singer did have sponsors and a clutch of devotees, he failed to make an impact on the commercial music world; in the country of his birth, he remained almost wholly unknown. It was rumored that he shot himself during a concert, or doused himself with kerosene and struck a match, or simply jumped to his death . . .

In South Africa, his music mattered greatly; he was, said one of his admirers, "bigger than Elvis," and his lyrics powered the antiapartheid movement as a kind of anthem of resistance. Hundreds of thousands sang his songs; no one knew the details of his life. Some years ago two fans of the performer set out to learn the truth of his death and found, to their astonishment, Rodriguez had survived. For decades he'd eked out a living as a construction and demolition worker in Detroit. He'd made no money from his album sales and had no knowledge that they sold; he had three daughters and an old guitar and no idea that half a world away he was a mythic figure, much revered.

*Searching for Sugar Man* reports on how the man was tracked down to his crumbling lair, then flown to Cape Town and Johannesburg, where he received a hero's welcome and performed to sold-out houses and adoring multitudes—unchanged. The hair still black, the pockmarked face still suggestive of an Aztec warrior, the hands still nimble on the strings and ready, after anonymity, to sign autographs for hours—it was as though the forty intervening years made no difference in his stance. As in a fairy tale (think of Sleeping Beauty or Rip Van Winkle), the artist was restored.

We were born a month apart. In the time when I first heard Joan Baez, Leonard Cohen, Judy Collins, Bob Dylan, Odetta, and others, the music of Sugar Man vanished; now he's an emblem of survival and the power of devotion. His youth is shadowed by old age; his age reprises youth. His tour in the fall of 2012 took him from Michigan to California, from Ontario to British Columbia, from the Royal Festival Hall, in England, to Scotland and Ireland. His acolytes have raised Rodriguez from, if not the dead, the disappeared.

All of us have once been young; some of us grow old. Imagine if the youthful dead could revisit their own pasts—to see, as Sixto Rodriguez has done, what happened to their early work and if and in what way it has endured. John Keats wrote for his tombstone: "Here lies One Whose Name was writ in Water." He was wrong. Others, greatly vaunted, have had reputations dwindle and their ashes turn to dust. When Sugar Man emerged from his—it's fair to call it—*cave* in Detroit and blinkingly came out of hibernation to the spotlight's glare, he was awakened from a lifelong sleep and asked to sing again. I cite him at book's start because the image of an elderly performer striding out on stage reborn is part of the dear dream of youth: that it can continue. And though he's not my subject here, he hovers in the wings, an old man reenacting what he did decades before. What had been lost is found.

"Prodigy." According to the *Oxford English Dictionary,* the word has little to do with chronological age. Its first definition is "something extraordinary from which omens are drawn: an omen, a portent." The next usage is "an amazing or marvelous thing, *esp.* something out of the ordinary course of nature; something abnormal or monstrous." Only a much later meaning associates that "amazing or marvelous thing" with youth, describing it as "a person endowed with some quality which excites wonder: *esp.* a child of precocious genius." The words "precocity" and "prodigy" share no etymological root. By now, however, we routinely link the two. A prodigy is youthful; the prodigy at fifty seems a contradiction in terms.

Nor is such early achievement always and only artistic. There are prodigies in mathematics and skating, chess and foreign languages. "Prodigy" is the name of an English electronic dance music group and a computer service. To be "prodigal"—as in the Prodigal Son—is to be wasteful or extravagant; to be "prodigious" is to be "marvelous" but also "ominous, portentous." The word itself comes from the Middle English *"prodige"* or *"portent,"* from the Latin *"prodigium,"* and its first known use was in a chronicle in the year 1494: "Many wonderfull prodyges & tokyns were shewed in Englonde, as ye swellying or rysyng of the water of Thamys." We have traveled a fair distance from the notion of a rising tide to the notion of an artist in the first flush of youth.

The latter is my topic. *The Art of Youth* concerns itself with men and women—writers, painters, and musicians—dead before the age of forty. In one sense this is neither "out of the ordinary course of nature" nor "amazing" since many creative artists died by then and continue to do so today. They are legion in our history. Indeed, and though I've done no statistical survey, it's safe to say that most of our acknowledged masters completed their lives' labor by that age. The preponderance of what we honor as cultural achievements has been produced by the young. Much of this is a matter of actuarial tables and life expectancy; it's only in the recent past that forty years old *could* seem young. Two score was once a full life span; not now.

But my artists started quickly and were accomplished in their chosen fields by their early twenties. What they did, they did fully and soon. A separate inquiry might consider those who toil on with diminished effect or those who simply choose to stop, since not all creative labor ends with diminution or death. There are those in their sixties and eighties whose best work was done first. For the sake of coherence, however, I examine youthful figures whose talent was extinguished with their final breaths.

It goes without saying, but needs to be said, that all of what follows applies as well to other forms of endeavor — neuroscience and basketball, for instance, or prowess on the battlefield and in aerospace. There are many ways of starting out, many fields in which to flourish early — think of mathematics or philosophy or political reform. Such a discussion might instead have dealt with the gymnast or entrepreneur or inventor. The notion of "first acts" is one that cuts across the board and need not be delimited by a historical moment; it outstrips place and time.

Yet my focus is, as the title suggests, on art. I confine myself to writing, painting, and music because they are the imaginative modes of which I have firsthand knowledge. The same could equally be argued of what we call, in general, the "lively arts"; our culture has been everywhere shaped and sustained by the young. This book, however, is less a survey than analysis of one woman, two men, and their achievements. A fourth figure — that of the author — will make an appearance as well.

How best to describe the art of youth; when does it start, when stop? What "tokyns" and "portents" indicate the prodigy; how crucial a role does apprenticeship play? We take for granted, somehow, that athletic ability, physical agility, and sexual exuberance belong to the young body; what of the young mind? Is there a stage of age in which talent takes flight; what enables its adventures, and when and how do they end? Is the pattern always the same? The headlong rush of the opening act—the hurtling intensity of the beginner—does have risks attached. My artists each knew failure as well as important success. So is the secondary meaning of my title phrase a truthful or empty assertion; do we consider "the art of youth" a distinctive achievement or simply a function of age? Is there, I mean, some way of being a beginner that's not "wasted on the young"?

This book examines three creative personalities: a writer (Stephen Crane), a visual artist (Dora Carrington), and a musician (George Gershwin). Each was precociously gifted as well as prodigal; their trajectories were swift. One of my subjects died in his twenties; two lived till thirty-eight. Two succumbed to illness (one slowly advancing, one sudden); the third chose suicide. Two were American, one English; the first—the writer—was born in 1871, the last to die—the composer—did so in 1937. When Crane was young, America was in the painful aftermath of the Civil War; by the time of Gershwin's death, storm clouds had gathered for World War II.

Extraordinary as individuals, they nonetheless are representative figures. As artists they were innovative and as characters iconoclastic, standing apart from society's norms. None of them came from a family of practitioners or had been expected to make a life in art. Only the woman, Carrington, completed her studies in school. The painter distanced herself from the society she was born to; the writer died abroad. The composer stayed devoted to his family while traveling in social circles half a world away. Ambitious, all three sought recognition and, when it came, reacted strongly: Gershwin embraced the trappings of fame; Carrington withdrew. Stephen Crane did both.

People paid attention to these people, writing reminiscences, so their behavior can be monitored by an audience today. Self-invented, they broke rules — sexual as well as social — yet set standards for behavior in the years to come. Atypically for the period, the two men did not marry, and none of the trio had children (with the possible exception of an illegitimate child fathered by Gershwin). Companionship bulked large, however, in the lives of the writer and painter, and their consorts were notable; the composer too was known by the company he kept.

The difference in their histories is, however, finally as telling as the similarities. And that's an additional reason I picked these three out of the thirty or three hundred figures I might instead have discussed. Together they cover the terrain this book attempts to map. What they did and didn't do remains, I think, remarkable, and to delineate their efforts is to look collectively at the art of youth. Not every aspect of these histories entails increase and plenty; there's grief and loss here too. As with so many men and women cut off in their early prime, one asks the unanswerable question: What more might they have done? Unlike the drama of Sixto Rodriguez, my brief lives have no second acts. Yet the work survives.

# 1

## First Acts

"Then come kiss me, sweet and twenty,
Youth's a stuff will not endure . . ."

— WILLIAM SHAKESPEARE, *Twelfth Night*

IN LASTINGNESS: THE ART OF OLD AGE (2011), I wrote of musicians, painters, and writers who worked till the end of their natural lives, and whose lives were long. They maintained and even advanced their creative enterprise past the age of seventy; think, for example, of Pablo Casals, Thomas Hardy, Georgia O'Keeffe, Pablo Picasso, Giuseppe Verdi, and William Butler Yeats. It seems self-evident that those who live extended lives will know some things they once did not; time is the currency with which we pay for incremental understanding of the distant view. Perspective does increase.

Starting out is not the same; we cannot tell for certain how long we will persist. By now I have been publishing books for nearly half a century, and to begin with I could not imagine what it means to keep keeping on. At twenty-three, when my first book appeared, I was sure some sort of Halley's Comet would signal its arrival and everything would change. Today I understand, of course, that nothing of that order happens; nuclear annihilation remains a threatful possibility, and starvation and disease are problems not redressed by art (or in any case not by mine). To add a painting or a melody or a novel to the stock of those available is not to save the world.

Yet there's still a small *frisson* of expectation: What next? The winner's circle always beckons; the stirrup cup awaits. It seems to me the youthful maker *must* believe in the importance of what she or he makes; else how or why continue? There's no foregone conclusion or retrospect involved in the prospect of a career; in our beginning is our end, perhaps, but the creative personality sees no easy outside limit to what he or she will attain. To live one's life as an artist is to dream of immortality. *I leave you this picture, this poem, this song* is the young person's clarion call, and though there's rarely an answering cry, it may sometimes echo awhile.

"Late style" is a topic now current; from Rudolf Arnheim to Harold Bloom, from Edward Said to Helen Vendler, it has become the subject of critical discussion. Early expressiveness has been less often considered—as though it were coeval with the start of a career and therefore unremarkable, a necessary precondition of the work. But first acts too are crucial; beyond the pure pleasure of making, they predict the size and contour of any achievement to come. And when no further achievements exist, first acts are all we have.

Consider the poets Byron, Keats, and Shelley, or the composers Mendelssohn, Mozart, and Schubert. None of these towering figures attained the age of forty; Keats died at twenty-five. The list of those who can properly be called precocious—Thomas Chatterton dead at seventeen, Jean-Michel Basquiat at twenty-seven, Théodore Géricault at thirty-two—is long. Between the 1890s and the 1920s, think of Guillaume Apollinaire, Henri Gaudier-Brzeska, Rupert Brooke, Henri de Toulouse-Lautrec, Katherine Mansfield, Wilfred Owen, Georges Seurat, Vincent van Gogh, and too many others to name; not one reached a fortieth year. Even the descriptive term "old masters" points to the period of production and not to the age of the maker; the painters Caravaggio, Giorgione, Raphael—to take just three examples from the Italian Renaissance—expired in their thirties. Insofar as his dates have been with certainty established, the painter we know as Masaccio (1401–1427?) was dead at twenty-six.

On September 9, 1513, when he was seventeen months old, James V became King of Scotland. James VI received that title even younger, at thirteen months, on July 24, 1567. In 1603, at the venerable age of thirty-seven, he succeeded Queen Elizabeth I and became James I of England—which he then ruled for twenty-two years. Louis XIV, the Sun King, succeeded his father at the age of four years and eight months; his country at that time had nineteen million people, and he "owned" their bodies as well as their property. Pope Benedict IX, when twelve, assumed the position of pontiff in 1032, the youngest in the history of the Roman Catholic Church. The current Dalai Lama was enthroned in Tibet at the age of five, in 1940; he remains the spiritual leader of his people although in exile from his homeland and unable to return. K'ang Hsi became Emperor of China in 1661 when he was not yet seven years old. He reigned thereafter for sixty-one years, with three empresses who presented him with thirty-five sons of his own. Power—at least in its titular and inherited guise—can come soon.

But what of power that is neither self-anointed nor appointed? Let me start with literature, since of the three modes in my study it's verbally expressive and can describe the problem. As William Butler Yeats proclaims, perhaps a touch too loudly, "I have drunk ale from the Country of the Young / And weep because I know all things now." In "A Defense of Poetry" (1821), Percy Bysshe Shelley asserts that "poets are the unacknowledged legislators of the world." His phrase too is hyperbolic, but what of those un-acknowledged legislators we call important writers; when does their reign begin?

To die in one's twenties or thirties is not necessarily to have been a beginner. The poet—or the musician or painter—may well confront mortality at an early age. When T. S. Eliot has his titular character J. Alfred Prufrock declare, "I grow old . . . I grow old . . . I shall wear the bottoms of my trousers rolled," the writer himself was in his early twenties and his alter ego only a little older. The spinsters in Jane Austen's books are rarely more than thirty; when Shakespeare wrote his celebrated sonnet on old age ("That time of year thou may'st in me behold . . ."), he would have been what we consider young. The medical student John Keats, who recognized his own arterial blood while cough-ing, was no less aware of his physical decline than Walter Savage Landor writing "Memory" at ninety. When Patti Smith composed *Just Kids,* her companion Robert Mapplethorpe had died years be-fore—in his mid-forties—of AIDS.

Mortality has been a topic for painters, writers, and musicians all along. But life that ends at twenty is a different thing than life terminated at eighty, and many of our culture's masterworks have focused on the former. A death that arrives in the fullness of time is less often the subject of elegiac lament than death that seems premature; from Achilles on Patroclus to John Milton on young Edward King, the literature of mourning deals with a lover or a friend "dead ere his prime." (Near the start of his great elegy, Milton puts it this way: "For Lycidas is dead, dead ere his prime, / Young Lycidas, and hath not left his peer . . .") When Edgar Allan Poe (1809–1849) composed "The Raven" or wrote grievingly of "Annabel Lee," he was lamenting the loss of a maiden, not a mother or grandmother; in the various fables and myths where Death comes to claim a prized lady, it's predictably a beautiful virgin, not crone, he carries off as prize. And when a life is over soon, the speculations on *what if* seem almost unavoidable, as though a second act might plausibly have followed with a second roll of dice.

A number of our gifted young die early and by accident as well as choice: the rule of time and chance. Had Wilfred Owen not been shot in the First World War, or Christopher Marlowe knifed in a tavern, their poetic output no doubt would have enlarged. Had Sylvia Plath or Hart Crane been medicated in the modern fashion, they might not have grown suicidal but rather continued to write. We know *their* names, but not the nameless multitudes of poets-soon-to-publish who instead have been consigned to unmarked graves. The musician with a racking cough or painter with consumption is nearly a stereotype of *la vie bohème;* think of all those figures on the opera stage or movie screen who address the score or sketch pad while the clock approaches midnight and their faces go cadaverous . . .

In this sense, early death is a central motif of the human condition, and one of the great topics of the tribe. From Andrew Marvell's "To His Coy Mistress" to Dylan Thomas's "Do Not Go Gentle into That Good Night," our poetry instructs us: *Carpe diem*—seize the day. The lament "In Time of Pestilence," by Thomas Nashe (who died at thirty-four, in 1601), contains this fearsome stanza:

> Beauty is but a flower
> Which wrinkles will devour;
> Brightness falls from the air;
> Queens have died young and fair;
> Dust hath closed Helen's eye;
> I am sick, I must die—
>> Lord, have mercy on us!

• • •

That children love to draw and paint is a near-universal truth; the crayon and the coloring book are everyday enchantments. To walk into a preschool gathering or kindergarten class is to witness a triumph of color and shape; by junior high and high school the walls look less alive. The walls of lecture halls at the college and postgraduate levels are almost totally blank. Outsider art and folk art (as well as that of artists deemed insane) tends to blur those boundaries; the style of the few who stay innocent-eyed retains the feel and flavor of inspired play. For most of us, however, youthful inventiveness fades. Why this should be the case—a diminished willingness in adults to toy with light and lines and clay—is almost as much a mystery as the reverse: why some of those children persist.

Still, there's a limit to the excellence of kindergarten paintings, no matter how unlimited the joy. And it's fair to say, I think, that even the gifted young artist must be tutored in the skills of rendering and representation; no one first handles the chisel or the paintbrush with, as it were, perfect pitch. Apprenticeship has always been part of the process of growth, and perhaps the crucial distinction between those who improve and those who put their paint boxes away is the willingness to welcome such apprenticeship—to get better at drawing a human figure or a distant tree. To try again, again, *again* and not grow bored or angry is to enter the profession (or to succumb to the lure of it) at an early age.

So how do gifts declare themselves; how do we recognize and, thereafter, measure them? What constitutes a prodigy and what is mere precocity; where does one draw the line? The child playing Czerny exercises or reciting nursery rhymes to an audience of adults is a stock figure, nearly, and most parents think their son or daughter is special. Little Bob with his drum set or Babs in her tutu seem particularly gifted to the doting dad and mom. All those rainbows and smiley faces done with finger paint in kindergarten fairly clamor for a viewing on the refrigerator door. I don't mean to disparage this; I too believed our children and now our children's children were and are remarkable, each in their own way unique.

They are, of course; all human beings are one of a kind. No genetic pattern short of cloning precisely replicates another, and every mother's son and daughter is in fact unique. But DNA is one thing and precocious genius another; the child who hears the *St. Matthew Passion* and can retain it note for note is not the same as one who hums the melody of "Twinkle, Twinkle, Little Star." The young artist who can draw a perfect circle freehand (as Michelangelo Buonarroti is reputed to have done) is not the same as one who manages stick figures in front of a square house. A child prodigy does possess a kind of genius, if genius means having a quicker relation to the passage of time than that of ordinary mortals—a more rapid gift of comprehension and a skill set acquired with ease. John Stuart Mill learned Greek at three, Latin a little later; by the age of twelve he was adroit at logic and at sixteen an economist. When we call a child "a natural," we mean something of the same: an effortless-seeming acquisition of skills that others labor painfully to learn. What X needs to study hard and stitch together thread by thread arrives to Y whole cloth.

Music offers us, perhaps, the clearest case of such "effortless-seeming acquisition." The gift is declared early on. When children learn to sit and stand, then walk and talk, they navigate the world at an astonishing rate. Neurons fire; synapses expand; the rate of growth is exponential by comparison with an adult's accretion of skills. An infant acquires information minute by hour and day by week; in a grown-up the process slows down. For the elderly it can reverse. And though I know of no governing series of genes, it does appear that certain individuals—a small and rare minority—acquire the language of music the way other children learn speech. It is as if the motor skills most people use to walk and talk are extended in the prodigy's brain to learning chords and scales. They would seem to listen to some unspoken set of instructions, hearing what we used to call "the music of the spheres" and knowing without conscious application which note must follow which. When they compose, it's almost as though they take dictation, copying; what they write, they write at speed.

How else to explain the youthful achievements of Palestrina or the work of J. S. Bach? How else to explain the early symphonies of Mozart or Mendelssohn's octet? Often this nature is nurtured; the children of musicians seem to have inherited an interest in and aptitude for the family trade. Often the training comes early; the fathers of Franz Liszt and Clara Wieck, to take just a pair of examples, urged their offspring on. In a house where music looms large, musical expressiveness may find a fertile ground.

Yet it still feels otherworldly when a prodigy comes out onstage to offer a performance. Here the word edges up against the dictionary definition of "amazing or marvelous"; the young Claudio Arrau and Yehudi Menuhin playing the piano and the violin did so in ways that beggar understanding. This is not the same as starstruck parents encouraging their darlings to perform in school recitals or *The Nutcracker;* it's as if some inner enabling power has taken these artists in hand. How is it *possible,* we ask ourselves, that they should have such physical dexterity or be able to remember all those notes? As I write, I've just finished watching a YouTube clip of a three-year-old towheaded maestro conducting the fourth movement of a recording of Beethoven's Fifth Symphony; he wields his baton with perfect precision and unalloyed delight.

In painting too it's often, if not always, a function of homeschooling. Pieter Bruegel the Elder, Lucas Cranach the Elder, Jacopo Bellini, and the rest no doubt expected their sons to enter in the studio, then guild. In the case of mercantile trades—basket weaving, plumbing, tile installation, and the like—we're unsurprised when the son accompanies his father at labor, the daughter her mother while fashioning lace. These are stereotypes, of course, and gender-patterned expectations, but it's nonetheless true that particular crafts were and often still are passed along from generation to generation. *My people have always built boats* is not in essence different than the kapellmeister's assumption his children will join the chorale. It's a family legacy, a family tradition, and those who make mosaics or carpets or symphonies may well commence at home.

The circus acrobat starts young; so do the Olympic swimmer and the equestrienne. The guitarist and the fashion model may well commence careers in their teens, and nowadays a mogul might be in his or her twenties—think Facebook, Microsoft, Oracle, YouTube, and the rest. The season's fresh new face and ingénue, the publishing phenom and rookie of the year all share a rapid arrival. *The next big thing, the breakthrough discovery*—our television programs celebrate first acts.

There are forms of quick achievement and identity that are, of course, unhappy ones: think child soldier or child prostitute, and it's clear precocity need not be glad or good. To be robbed of one's youth is all too often the fate of the poor and downtrodden; there are early elders everywhere who wish time might have slowed. To be "wise beyond one's years" is more likely than not to be unhappy or deprived. Yet by and large in Western culture we think sooner is better and soonest is best; the early bird gets the worm. A stitch in time saves nine. There's a joke about procrastination—"Why put off till tomorrow what you can postpone till the following day?"—and the not-so-implicit attitude toward the idea of *mañana* is that it's a lazy person's way to pass the time.

Instant gratification is, by contrast, something to be wished for; think of all the ways we have of saying "fast." "Two shakes of a lamb's tail," "lickety-split," "in the blink of an eye," "Speedy Gonzalez," "wicked quick"—such phrases indicate the rising star will plausibly be young. And given this general attitude—never too rapid and never too soon—it's unsurprising that in twenty-first-century society we put a premium on youthful demeanor and looks. Not so long ago we honored our elders and placed them stage center; now they're in retirement communities and nursing homes or having face-lifts and hair transplants and tummy tucks. Off camera and off the record, we still may equate old age with sagacity; on camera and on the record, we look for new talent and "original" ideas. Ecclesiastes informs us that "to everything there is a season," but to the promoter it's always, only, spring.

Our word "generation" is oxymoronic, suggesting both the inception of life and the slow passage of time. This is true of "commencement" as well; at graduation ceremonies things both begin and end. Our life patterns, as many have argued, are circular as well as linear; the "second childhood" of the ancient individual resembles infancy in ways too familiar to list. If the one-year-old and centenarian share a lack of language and motor skills, if "toothless" describes them both, then why not link the beginner and those who near an end? When William Wordsworth writes that infants come "trailing clouds of glory," he's being more than pious; there's a whole lifetime's worth of achievement locked up in that small bundle and waiting for release. A rapt devotion to color and clay, a pleasure in nursery rhyming and drums—the apparatus of self-expression is with us, if inchoate, early on.

All this has to do with a learning curve's speed. The goddess Athena, according to myth, sprang full-blown from the brain of Zeus—but the daughter of an Olympian is, almost by definition, unnatural; mere mortals take time to grow. Even Pablo Picasso—who liked to cultivate the notion that he was self-taught—began his studies under the close supervision of his artist-father. While other boys were climbing trees or kicking soccer balls, he stayed inside sharpening pencils; his tutelage was strict. So, once again, if we define the prodigy as someone with a different ratio to the passage of time than that of ordinary humans, the prodigy as artist is someone who learns fast.

If you add "fast" to "early," you have the art of youth. Impatience and intensity—those twinned components of ambition—spur the young maker on. "Cut is the branch that might have grown full straight," as Marlowe writes of Faustus, "and burned is Apollo's laurel bough . . ." That bustling rush with which the child completes a canvas or a melody or a story is insufficient proof of talent, perhaps, but a frequent marker: first efforts come, by and large, quick.

• • •

*Youth has no age.*—Pablo Picasso
*Youth is something very new. Twenty years ago,*
*no one mentioned it.*—Coco Chanel
*If youth knew; if age could.*—Sigmund Freud
*The wine of youth does not always clear with advancing years;*
*sometimes it grows turbid.*—Carl Jung
*Fame is the thirst of youth.*—George Gordon, Lord Byron

*Bashfulness is an ornament to youth, but a reproach to old age.*
—Aristotle
*Everybody's youth is a dream, a form of chemical madness.*
—F. Scott Fitzgerald
*Age considers; youth ventures.* —Rabindranath Tagore
*Youth is the best time to be rich, and the best time to be poor.*
—Euripides
*What Youth deemed crystal, Age finds out was dew.*
—Robert Browning

• • •

Much art is romantic; artists are; the notion of bohemia has long been linked with a kind of behavioral freedom. By and large the art of youth entails a risk-taking bravado; the creative person (or so we imagine) lives life at society's edge. Drink and drugs are part of it, as are "loose" morals and the revolutionary impulse and social/sexual experimentation. When Théophile Gautier wore a crimson vest or Isadora Duncan donned a diaphanous scarf, it was more than just a fashion statement. The marches and the rallies of gay and lesbian and transgender activists look jubilantly colorful and sound unabashedly loud.

This in-your-face aspect of liberation is one of the hallmarks of public display; *épater le bourgeois* was a stated aim of the Decadent poets in nineteenth-century France. Charles Baudelaire waved that banner; so did Paul Verlaine and his teenage lover, the astonishing Arthur Rimbaud. To "walk down Piccadilly with a poppy or a lily," as did W. S. Gilbert's caricature of Oscar Wilde, or to stroll the Boulevard Saint-Germain with a lobster on the leash is to "shock the bourgeois." "Don't trust anyone over thirty" is a more modern version of the same idea. Young Icarus who flew too high—defying the instructions of that master maker, his father—is an emblem both of youthful aspiration and the risks attached. If we disobey our parents, we may first soar, then fall.

All rules have exceptions, and this one does too; not every artist delights in confrontation or goes to transgressive extremes. Many save their daring for their art. Joris-Karl Huysmans, the author of that "decadent" text *À Rebours* (1884), behaved more like a stockbroker than a revolutionary. And the children of the middle class—among them Edgar Degas and Paul Cézanne, Gustave Flaubert and Robert Louis Stevenson—defy their parents' expectations at some cost. To give up a career in medicine or law is not always to embrace a mistress and a scarlet waistcoat; by all accounts Degas and Cézanne were thoroughly conventional in their private lives. Flaubert remained his mother's son and Stevenson indebted to his father no matter how far they roamed. Malcolm Lowry, the wild dipsomaniac, was a remittance man; till the end of his life he took money from his family in Liverpool, whose cotton-brokering business he scorned.

Again, it's Icarus who's emblematic here. The "old artificer" Daedalus (so described by James Joyce in the last lines of *A Portrait of the Artist as a Young Man*) survived his son and, mourning him, became an example of the classical, not romantic, figure. He valued order, not disruption; he wanted to keep things intact. The senior's style was that of power-in-reserve, the junior's that of power-on-display. In Friedrich Nietzsche's acute distinction from *On the Genealogy of Morals* (1887), the labyrinth-maker's art is Apollonian, his son's Dionysian. The first of these figures endorses restraint; the second embodies release. First acts are more likely to belong to the latter than former aesthetic; romance, though not exclusively, attaches to the young. What I'm trying to suggest is how, in a bourgeois society, the youthful creative talent stands most often in a kind of opposition to established norms, and how that very opposition can be self-defining. To assert oneself as painter, writer, and musician is at least in part to stake a claim: *I can fly higher than you . . .*

In earlier societies such contrariety seems less obvious; youthful artisans were members of guilds. In Greece or the medieval court a craftsman would be trained and thereafter expected to serve as goldsmith, harpist, or bard. Young women learned the piano and embroidery as part of their preparation for marriage; to sing or sketch was a domestic skill. And those aristocrats who painted, played, or wrote for their private amusement did so with no expectation of payment or public reward. The *career* of artist was, it seems to me, less often self-selected in previous times; you either were raised to be part of a guild or engaged in it for fun. It was either a profession in the mode of plasterer and weaver or an amateur's pursuit.

But since the nineteenth century (and, in many cases, earlier: think of Peter Paul Rubens or Antonio Vivaldi), the professional creator chooses that mode of expression as a way to make a living as well as live a life. Our supreme poet and playwright, William Shakespeare, deployed his skills with language to become a man of property. On his return home to Stratford, he made a show of wealth. Even the man or woman of independent means is likely to go public with the artifact produced. And though the odds are long, they're by no means insurmountable; we have daily evidence of money made in art.

When that happens, it too can be sexy, a subset and repository of the American dream. The young successful artist—like the athlete or entertainer—enters a charmed circle and goes to the head of the class. In a publicity-fueled cycle we learn constantly of "prodigies" who demonstrate achievement at an early age. And the earlier the better; think of the very young Tiger Woods driving golf balls in front of the camera, Michael Jackson and the Jackson 5, Shirley Temple with her curls. Elizabeth Taylor performed (with her ballet class) before King George V and Queen Mary at the age of three. The teenage skateboarder, the child saxophonist, or the young actress has the advantage over his or her elders if only as a novelty and the season's news.

Yet almost without exception we are made aware of success stories, not those of failure. The ones who never make it to the top are not on view. We know about men raised up by their bootstraps now living in mansions and driving fast cars. We join fan clubs of women once on the edge of poverty who have problems with addiction and the IRS. So we learn about their dreams and troubles, their romantic and business partners; we read about them online and in tabloids: grist to the rumor mill once they have names. Of the hundreds of singers and writers now silent, the thousands of athletes now weak-kneed and addled, we hear only distantly, rarely; it's the winner who takes all. The nameless don't get noticed or discussed.

Great talent, great intelligence, great good looks or luck may propel an artist forward; they do not guarantee a happy run. And the chronicle of early achievement—consider football players and computer programmers—includes a long listing of those who go wrong. Would Dylan Thomas, dead at thirty-nine, have drunk himself to death so rapidly if he had stayed unrecognized

in his fishing village in Wales? Would Jim Morrison or Kurt Cobain have ended their brief lives so soon if acolytes weren't waiting backstage with a needle or a glass? Would Egon Schiele, dead
of influenza at the age of twenty-eight, somehow have escaped
that plague if he'd been self-protective and walled off from society? These are rhetorical questions that can nonetheless be asked:
Does the art of youth entail its own extinction in the very act
of creation, a male praying mantis or female Chinook salmon
doomed to spawn and die?

Gustav Mahler commenced writing music at four, Sergei Prokof-
iev at five. The early minuets of Wolfgang Amadeus Mozart—
also composed at five years old—show a mastery of form; by the
age of six he was touring Europe, giving recitals on the clavier
and violin. Richard Strauss and Jacques Offenbach, at six, were
playing the violin and clavier and had written their first songs;
at seven Frédéric Chopin composed the Polonaise in G Minor
and, at twelve, gave a command performance for the tsar. César
Franck, born in Belgium, entered the Liège Conservatory at the
age of eight; Franz Liszt began composing at eight, and a year
later made his debut appearance on the concert stage. Georges
Bizet was studying composition at the Paris Conservatory at nine,
and Béla Bartók produced his first dance pieces at that age. Felix
Mendelssohn and Clara Wieck Schumann began their performing careers when nine, and Niccolò Paganini, the Italian virtuoso
of the violin, made a concert appearance at ten. By eleven, Ludwig van Beethoven was assistant to the court organist Christian
Neefe, and at the same age Robert Schumann composed a setting
of Psalm 150.

The list goes on. Youthful prowess—at least in the world of musicians—is, although remarkable, not rare. The child in short pants or a pinafore who steps out on the concert stage and picks up a stringed instrument or settles on a piano stool is almost a familiar sight, and particularly so if the family has been involved in the profession. Indeed, the philosopher G.W.F. Hegel (1770–1831) denied that music is a serious art since so many children are so good at it; if a six- or eight-year-old can compose and perform, he argued, how important can any such achievement be? He was, no doubt, nonmusical, and had a tin ear.

Notable precocity can be found elsewhere as well. In 1665, at age twenty-two, Isaac Newton developed the binomial theorem and differential calculus; the next year he set forth the theory of colors, integral calculus, and the law of universal gravitation. James Watson was twenty-five when he and Francis Crick read the genetic code and identified the double helix shape of DNA. Guglielmo Marconi was twenty-seven in 1901 when he transmitted radiotelegraphy signals across the Atlantic. Albert Einstein, who had seemed a backward child, wrote an essay at sixteen that contained the germ of his special theory of relativity. The breakthrough work of mathematicians, physicists, and inventors is very often accomplished at or near career's start. This is a separate issue, but it seems also true that, *absent* such rapid achievement, a life's work won't amount to much; the mathematician who declares a vocation at forty is a rare creature indeed. As with tennis, ballet, or gymnastics, it's a practice best embarked upon when young.

Jane Austen wrote her novel *Elinor and Marianne* when nineteen, in 1795. It was published anonymously some sixteen years later, as *Sense and Sensibility.* Mary Shelley — at the prompting of her husband's friend Lord Byron — composed and published *Frankenstein* in 1818, at the age of twenty. Charles Dickens became the most successful author in Great Britain at twenty-five with his comic serial novel *The Pickwick Papers* (1837). At the same age, in 1821, John Keats — he of the unequalled ear for music in the English language — died.

I can think of no visual artist — with the possible exception of such "primitives" as Henri Rousseau and Grandma Moses — who did not start early. This is not to say that Thomas Gainsborough, Édouard Manet, Nicolas Poussin, Leonardo da Vinci, and the rest did their best painting as beginners, but their apprentice work does herald the accomplishment of mid- and late career. In the contemporary art scene a painter with her first exhibition at forty might well be called a late bloomer; the rainbow arc of "visibility" often has its starting point when an artist emerges from school.

Here it's worth repeating that the numbers themselves have changed. As a species we've grown gray. When Ludwig van Beethoven was in his mid-fifties, he had outlived the life expectancy of his contemporaries in Vienna by almost a decade; when Lord Byron died at thirty-six, he was — in actuarial terms — only a few years younger than his generation's standard age at death. William Shakespeare died in his early fifties, but given the life span of those born in the sixteenth century, he cannot be described as in his prime. Rembrandt van Rijn, who died at sixty-three, was elderly, if not ancient; so was Johann Sebastian Bach at sixty-five. There were always statistical outliers, artists such as Michelangelo, Sophocles, and Titian, who lived very long lives. But octogenarians and nonagenarians were the exception, no rule; most artists would have completed their work well before the age of forty, now our baby boomers' age. These days we say, "They were too young," when we learn of people dead at sixty-five or seventy; a century ago that statement would have seemed absurd.

So the "middle game"—to use a chess term—might well begin at twenty. If you apprentice to a craft at twelve, you get your walking papers some seven years thereafter; if you play your first concert by seven or nine, it's unsurprising that by twenty-five you're an "old" musical hand. Growth in our modern world is both more rapid and more deferred. The paradox of quick independence—the coddled child with credit cards and cell phone, the teenage star with handlers—is perhaps not all that different in kind from the situation of those potentates I listed above. The Sun King at four and pontiff at twelve were surely not responsible for the daily management of realm or church; their titular duties were nonetheless in place. The history of performance is filled with wage earners in their teens, and royalty can be conferred—think of Taylor Swift or Justin Bieber—by a large royalty check.

There are, it seems to me, three kinds of first acts to describe.

1. A creative man or woman who starts fast and well and is "cut off untimely" due to circumstance or what we used to call fate. These include the multitude lost to disease and war, the artists who might have continued to grow had they continued to work. In statistical terms, indeed, these folk are the rule, not the exception; only in our recent history and in the "developed" world do most of us live long. During the Roman Empire and the Pax Romana, the average citizen's

life span is thought to have been twenty-eight; as recently as 1900, the average life expectancy was a mere forty-five. In the case of this cadre, moreover, the question of "what might have been" remains unanswerable: what they leave is what we know. What they made is what we have.

2. A man or woman who starts early and proves self-destructive. These include both accidental deaths and those that are self-engendered, as well as those who simply choose to leave the stage. In our present time the young performer is most adored when most at risk; the recklessness that wrecks them often is part of the act. A common denominator here has to do with exuberance, an explosive energy that can become implosive; these youthful talents share a sense that there's no point in planning for tomorrow. In this category it's fair to raise the question of the squandering of gifts, the stewardship — or lack thereof — of talent early on. *What if* does enter in.

3. An artist who does his or her best work young, then falters. Here the diminution is neither a function of bad luck nor of timing but what we might call "character"; the habit of expressiveness remains intact, with nothing left to express. Consider Hemingway or Faulkner, and how our sense of their achievement would have altered had they died at forty, with the bulk of the great work accomplished. A few creative personalities choose to spend their final years away from the easel or desk. Charles Ives devoted his attention to actuarial tables, and Gioachino Rossini to the dining table; Marcel Duchamp played chess. Arthur Rimbaud, that prodigy, ceased serious writing in his teens and said, in effect,

*Ca suffit:* Enough's enough. The artist's life is not in such cases confined to an opening arc, but the early work is what counts.

In order to keep this discussion at manageable length, I confine myself in principal part to the first of these three categories. (I limit myself also to examples from the Western world; to deal with other cultures is to venture far afield.) One could write about the waning of talent, the Muse's long and sad farewell, the pitfalls and the pratfalls a performer must avoid. It's tempting, indeed, to consider the many reasons beyond the merely chronological that the art of youth—so vivid once—might falter, and its inventiveness fade. But, as I report in Chapter 5, the critic Cyril Connolly did so in *Enemies of Promise,* and his account is so exhaustive that the best I could muster is paraphrase; that excellent analysis stays relevant today. Suffice it here to say that what happens to young talent beyond the age of forty is not my subject now.

The next three chapters deal, in chronological order, with Stephen Crane, Dora Carrington, and George Gershwin. The data and the details of their careers are explored hereafter, but why, in effect, should I focus on *them* and not those countless others who would qualify as subjects by virtue of early achievement? In part this has to do with the degree of their eminence; their names are recognizable, but their stories not so familiar as to need no retelling. Gershwin is, I'd venture, the best known of this trio, Carrington the least, and Crane remembered by most readers for a single text.

To write of Mozart or Keats or Caravaggio is to have nothing new to report; their achievements have been often analyzed. But to write of unknown artists, no matter how prodigious, would be to skirt the issue of success. In part, as well, I wanted figures close to our own historical moment yet sufficiently removed so perspective can be gained; they are *of* our time and place, though not precisely *in* it, and we have the advantage of hindsight when assessing their careers. The world they worked and played in is a world not all that separate from the one we at present inhabit, and the issues with which they were wrestling remain with us today.

Since none of my subjects reached forty, the last of the three categories listed is the least pertinent. Yet the trajectory of their talent was by no means a straight upward line; in some respects, both Crane and Carrington entered a downward spiral at life's end. And Gershwin was so resolutely various in his endeavors that it's hard to imagine him writing, say, *Porgy and Bess: The Sequel*. That they did not live till forty is somehow unsurprising; theirs was vitality exhausted, not conserved. What they would have done in older age is impossible to know.

Still, insofar as one can categorize, George Gershwin represents the first of my three categories, Dora Carrington the second, and Stephen Crane the third. The first was "cut off untimely"; the second proved self-negating; the third worked to diminished effect. Even these distinctions, however, feel ragged-edged, not neat; it could well be argued that each of these brief lives contains a component of all three varieties of a first act. The categories overlap. So what we'll mostly notice is the difference in their stories, yet all three artists embody a problem this book will explore: What are the markers of early achievement, and how can it best be sustained?

Think of how we deal with youthful talent, the set of responses to those who begin: encouragement, exhortation, extravagant applause. And then the cool assessing gaze, a series of critiques. What the adult as role model does is to establish goals to pursue, and then to keep raising the bar. The three artists I here profile were, to a considerable extent, self-taught, and it's difficult to know the moment they left their teachers behind. Crane, Carrington, and Gershwin each emerge from contexts both cultural and instructional, but what one notices about them is their swift absorption of the lessons learned. These three were nothing if not independent, and originality was with them from the start.

A separate calculus applies to the young woman or man who consciously faces a premature death. (Crane knew, it seems, he was going to die; Gershwin had no such knowledge; Carrington took her own life.) Franz Schubert in his final year must certainly have been aware he was ill and unlikely to recover; the great outpouring of music has an urgency compounded by the prospect of collapse. Those soaring melodies could not, I think, have been composed by someone with no sense of his own approaching end. In this regard, perhaps, the age of the creative artist has less to do with her or his achievement than does the number of years left to live. Here it's less a matter of how old than how far from extinction. Those aphoristic observations quoted in this chapter, from Pablo Picasso to Robert Browning—the former dead in his nineties, the latter in his late seventies—proceed from a kind of self-congratulatory aloofness: the smug conviction on the speaker's part that he or she has survived to tell the tale.

A cautionary note: The biographer or critic runs the risk of teleology and retroactive projection. We must not attempt to deduce, from the vantage of life's close, how things seemed at the start; all of us are born to die, yet very few acknowledge that utter statistical certainty as we settle down to work. The deaths of Crane, Carrington, and Gershwin figure largely in my narrative but only terminally in theirs; *we* know the end of these stories, but their protagonists did not. The youthful artist is forward-facing, not retrospective, and when we try to imagine what this trio imagined, we must not imbue the narrative with, as it were, the sense of an ending; even Picasso and Browning, those honored elders of the tribe, had no clear sense of what would happen next.

Too, there's a distinction to draw between the young athlete and artist: the former knows that her or his career will be brief, with a finite span of years in which to make a mark; the latter has no such prior knowledge and may dream of "world enough and time." I can remember declaring, at twenty, that I had no idea *what* I'd be writing twenty years thereafter but was certain I'd be writing at that then-far-distant date. This turns out, happily, to have proved true, but I'm astonished now to know how blithe was that assertion and how blinkered the conviction that I could and would continue. It's a shaky assumption to make. Still, by and large the art of youth is based on the belief that there *will* be continuity; first acts derive in part from the enlivening delusion that the play goes on.

• • •

"There are no second acts in American lives," F. Scott Fitzgerald (1896–1940) declared. He proved himself wrong with his own final efforts; *Tender Is the Night* and the unfinished *The Last Tycoon* are infinitely more interesting than were his first two novels, *This Side of Paradise* and *The Beautiful and the Damned*. (In between, of course, and at the age of twenty-seven he wrote his masterful *The Great Gatsby*—but as he reports in "The Crack-Up," he did so at real cost.) The older and embittered author wrote books of an order of magnitude greater than that of the Jazz Age icon swallowing goldfish and jumping fully clothed into the fountain of the Plaza. His first act brought success and wealth; his second brought lasting achievement, though he felt both infirm and ignored. Still, Fitzgerald sounds more and more accurate now, his assertion increasingly true.

Ours is a culture committed to youth. We fear decline; we praise aspiration; the American dream consists of the future, not past. Though we're aging as a nation, we celebrate our children and the first flush of success. Death may well be, as Shakespeare writes, "the undiscovered country from whose bourne no traveler returns," but undiscovered country is the landscape each genuine artist traverses and from which art returns. And this has little or nothing to do, I think, with the traveler's age; the great discoveries exist outside of time. "Youth's a stuff will not endure," perhaps, but the art of youth may do so. It lives on.

# 2

## *Stephen Crane*

In the desert
I saw a creature, naked, bestial,
Who, squatting upon the ground,
Held his heart in his hands,
And ate of it.
I said: "Is it good, friend?"
"It is bitter—bitter," he answered;
"But I like it
Because it is bitter,
And because it is my heart."

— STEPHEN CRANE, *The Black Riders*

ON A JANUARY SUNDAY in 2012, I made my way to Hillside, New Jersey, and the Evergreen Cemetery where Stephen Crane lies buried. His stone is not easy to find. Had there been more than a dusting of snow, the tablet with his name incised would have been invisible: *Stephen Crane: Author, 1871–1900.* A grander upright plinth nearby lists names and dates of his large family, beginning with his father, Jonathan Townley Crane; then his mother, Mary Helen Peck Crane; and then his brothers and sisters. Here Stephen is described as *Poet-Author*, but takes no pride of place; the toppled marbles and the obelisks lay greater claim to attention, as do the cast-iron cannons pointing out at city streets.

The day was windy, cold. There's a certain stately dignity to cemeteries everywhere, and Evergreen does keep its grass close-cropped. But the site is ringed by auto body repair shops, pizza joints, and shuttered houses; on that Sunday morning, only a nearby Walgreens showed any signs of life. Hillside, once semirural, now is a suburb of Newark and battling with decay. It isn't a battle the township has won. One gate was open; the others were locked. A sign proclaimed that, since 1990, the budget for maintenance of the grounds has not included sufficient funds to tend to flowers or memorial urns.

There were, nonetheless, a few plastic floral tributes near the graves of loved ones; these were overturned by wind. A single car drove past. No other visitors came. Settling on an oak tree above a mausoleum labeled *Rogers,* crows cawed and preened and shat. The wind increased. I found myself remembering an epitaph from the *Greek Anthology:*

> In my nineteenth year the darkness drew me down.
> And ah, the sweet sun!

Crane lived till he was twenty-eight and had his share of sunlit days. But the darkness drew him irrevocably down, and there's a doubled irony in his few final letters. On the first day of the year, he wrote his landlord's son, Hugh Frewen: "Allow me to wish you a very fine shining 1900." And to an acquaintance on January 4 he inscribed the following: "A long 20th Century to you and yours."

For the writer, it was not.

His name was one to reckon with, a lineage to claim. "A Crane had sailed with Sir Francis Drake; another had been a member of the Massachusetts Bay Company, and still others had participated in the earliest settlement of Connecticut and New Jersey." Young Stephen was descended from a founder of the New Haven Colony, Jasper Crane; his own ancestral namesake had settled in New Jersey when New Jersey was a colony. There followed a succession of soldiers, ministers, and judges, and he would have learned this early on.

His father, a Methodist minister, was a presiding elder of the Newark district, his mother a good Methodist and advocate of temperance. Fourteen children were born to the Cranes; eight of his siblings lived past infancy. On November 1, 1871, Jonathan Townley Crane, D.D., wrote in his diary: "This morning at 5:30 our fourteenth child was born. We call him Stephen, the name of the ancestor of the Elizabethtown Cranes, who was one of the Company of 'Associates' who settled at E. town in 1665; also of S. Crane of Revolutionary times, who was prominent in patriotic labors and counsels for 15 years."

That forefather Stephen Crane was one of five New Jersey delegates to the First Continental Congress in 1774. A family housing development with their shared name adorning it exists in Newark still. As his first biographer, Thomas Beer, reports: "There were Cranes in the colony when Anne was queen of England; the Crane who figured in the Continental Congress had his coat armor painted on the flaps of his saddle bag. Plainly, the good and quiet baby was named with care."

Whether he was good and quiet is open to some question. The baby of the family, he proved himself both sickly and rambunctious; a spirit of adventure was with him from the start. A childhood friend, Post Wheeler, claimed that before the age of seven Crane was smoking Sweet Caporal cigarettes and drinking beer. Throughout his life he swung pendulum-like from exertion to exhaustion, and with a febrile energy; he was happy playing baseball; he loved dogs. Turn by turn, he read and rode. Twenty years thereafter, he described the first horse he sat on as vast—and how sternly, learning horsemanship, he was ordered not to cry. His brothers Edmund and Wilbur report on taking the five-year-old swimming and how he waded out into the current without fear or knowledge of staying afloat. Edmund remembers: "I plucked him out, gasping but unscared, just as his yellow hair was going under. We boys were naturally delighted with his grit." Crane's apprentice fictions, *Sullivan County Sketches*, deal with adventure and physical bravado: mountains and bears and fishing rods figure in them largely, and what fires the young man's imagination is, not atypically, risk.

Early on, "Stevie" wrote about his martial antecedents, including one ancestor who, "while proceeding to his father's bedside, was captured by some Hessians and upon his refusing to tell the road by which they intended to surprise a certain American outpost, they beat him with their muskets and then having stabbed him with their bayonets, they left him dead in the road."

These were scholarly people as well. Stephen's father, the Reverend Jonathan Townley Crane, graduated from the College of

New Jersey (later renamed Princeton University); his writings are both elegant and informal, on topics such as "A Talk about Talk, or The Art of Talking" (1868) and *Methodism and Its Methods* (1876). Mary Helen Peck Crane, his wife, was related to a bishop and one of the founders of Syracuse University; her writings include "How to Conduct a Weekly Meeting of the Woman's Christian Temperance Union" (1883). Stephen's favorite sister, Agnes, attended Wyoming Seminary (1872–1874) and Bound Brook Institute; she wrote poems and essays, as well as unsigned fictions, and was instrumental in encouraging him to read. Another sister, Mary Helen ("Nellie"), graduated from Pennington Seminary and Female Collegiate Institute (where the Reverend Mr. Crane had served for a decade as principal).

His siblings went to college, medical school, and law school, but the youngest child's experience of institutional learning was brief. He spent two years at Pennington Seminary, then left without a degree and, at sixteen, matriculated in a quasi-military academy at Claverack, New York. Claverack College did offer him a uniform and military instruction; some of the school's personnel had been soldiers in the Civil War, and their conversation may have furnished him with background for *The Red Badge of Courage*. Mostly, he smoked pipes, played sports, and chafed. "I never learned anything there," Crane would write. "But heaven was sunny blue and no rain fell on the diamond when I was playing baseball. I was very happy . . ."

Enrolled first at Lafayette College and then Syracuse University, he proved himself indifferent to formal education. Calling it a waste of time, and attending only a few lectures, he absorbed instead the lessons of the police station, law court, and back alleys. As he put it: "Humanity was a much more interesting study. When I ought to have been at recitations [at Syracuse] I was studying faces on the streets."

Central also to his sense of self was an enforced independence. It may not have been wholly welcome, yet Stevie had no choice. His father died of a heart attack at the age of sixty, when Crane was eight; his mother died ten years later, in 1891. Mary Helen Peck Crane, his mother, had suffered a series of nervous collapses; two of his brothers were alcoholics, and Stephen in his youth was often ill. His brother Luther died at twenty-three in 1886, as a result of a train accident (he had been a flagman); two years earlier, at twenty-eight, his beloved sister Agnes succumbed to cerebrospinal meningitis. (This is not to mention the five children Mrs. Crane had lost as infants, or brother Townley's two children, both of whom died young.) By the time he turned twenty, therefore, and with brother Edmund serving as his guardian, the baby of the family had little family left. It's surely not an accident that he clung to elder mentors (Hamlin Garland, William Dean Howells, Joseph Conrad, etc.) for much of his career, and that the woman who meant most to him (Cora Stewart) was in some ways a maternal presence, six full years his senior.

The Newark Crane was born in is not today a city he would recognize; the township of Hillside where he lies buried is scarcely, as in the name of its cemetery, evergreen. His stone (section C, lot 168) sits in New Jersey, yet he died in Badenweiler, Germany, where he'd gone in the hope of a cure for consumption; by that time he called England home. So the trajectory suggests both change and continuity: a rebel and a pioneer whose pedigree was long. Though he made his reputation as a chronicler of slums,

Crane had friends as well connected as Theodore Roosevelt and, later, Henry James. Throughout his life he wrangled with the parental dictates of religious faith and temperance, to neither of which he himself subscribed. The tenets of the family were with him in absentia, however, and while he wandered restlessly, he stayed in touch with those he'd left behind. It's no small part of his pattern of behavior that "those he'd left behind" were no longer his nearest and dearest; at a very early age, Crane lost the sense of protective enclosure a close-knit clan provides.

As a writer too he veered between high seriousness and hackwork; it sometimes seems as though there were *two* Stephen Cranes. One of them was an ambitious and committed artist, the other a war correspondent with a for-hire pen. One wrote poetry; the other met deadlines for cash. Till the very end he composed rapidly and overmuch; his final effort, *The O'Ruddy,* was slapdash, if not ill-conceived. There's a sense, throughout, of the author attempting to focus on some large creative challenge — then dissipating focus while waiting for that challenge to arrive. As he wrote in *War Is Kind:*

> A man said to the universe:
> "Sir, I exist!"
> "However," replied the universe,
> "The fact has not created in me
> A sense of obligation."

All this is to suggest a vivid presence engaged in autoerasure. The dominant mode of his language is surely that of irony, and distance is a precondition of the ironical stance. It offers one good reason his enigmatic figure has proved, for biographers, so hard to pin down; he was a mass of contradictions—self-acknowledged, self-aware. *The Correspondence of Stephen Crane* remains the central source of information about his personal behavior, but the letters themselves are often cryptic and rarely self-disclosing. As he confessed to an admirer: "Ye Gods! I am clay—very common uninteresting clay. I am a good deal of a rascal, sometimes a bore, often dishonest." And to his editor, Ripley Hitchcock, he wrote: "I cannot help vanishing and disappearing and dissolving. It is my foremost trait."

In the summer of 1888, the sixteen-year-old Stephen went to work for brother Townley, collecting newspaper stories for Townley's press bureau at Asbury Park. Shortly thereafter he became the Syracuse correspondent for the *New York Tribune,* and his first published writings were articles such as "Asbury's New Move," printed in the *Philadelphia Press,* then a string of unsigned pieces for the *Asbury Park Journal* and the *New York Tribune.* For several seasons the younger Crane provided newspaper material on the daily life of New Jersey; it would be his launching pad for the alleys and slums of New York. The dispatches are clear, the eye a noticing one; his apprenticeship was served out on the streets.

He had been writing since childhood. At four years old he was composing poetry, and his first known short story, "Uncle Jake and the Bell Handle," was produced at the age of fourteen. Still, the early work, while promising, gives no indication of artistic mastery. These efforts suggest a comfort with and interest in language, not the prodigious achievement of, say, Keats or

Chatterton. A schoolboy humor characterizes the *Sullivan County Sketches;* the satiric style is congenial to Crane.

All this began to change. To his inamorata Lily Brandon Munroe, he would later write (on February 29, 1896):

> You know, when I left you . . . I renounced the clever school in literature. It seemed to me that there must be something more in life than to sit and cudgel one's brains for clever and witty expedients. So I developed all alone a little creed of art which I thought was a good one. Later I discovered that my creed was identical with the one of Howells and Garland and in this way I became involved in the beautiful war between those who say that art is man's substitute for nature and we are the most successful in art when we approach the nearest to nature and trust, and those who say — well, I don't know what they say . . .

That "little creed of art" is what we've come to call American Realism, or Naturalism. Replete with detail and an attitude of seeming objectivity, it chronicles the mores of the workaday world. The influence of the environment on human character and destiny takes stage center. Nurture is much more important than nature; people behave as they must, not as they should. It follows therefore that the ugly underbelly of society comes under scrutiny, and the grim imperatives of (mostly urban) life are painstakingly described.

The then-current champions of this form of "approach the nearest to nature" were, as his letter attests, William Dean Howells and Hamlin Garland. Crane admired the "Dean of American

Letters" unreservedly. Of the work of Howells he wrote: "*A Modern Instance* is the greatest, most rigidly artistic novel ever written by an American, and ranks with the great novels of the world. *A Hazard of New Fortunes* is the greatest, sanest, truest study of a city in fiction." And Hamlin Garland welcomed him as protégé; theirs was the university in which the young artist enrolled. Both of them endorsed his credo of plain-style documentation. Not for Crane the ornamental speech or rhetorical tropes of the then-prevailing wind.

To a twenty-first-century reader, however, the prose of his debut effort still seems overwrought. In *Maggie: A Girl of the Streets,* a writer acquires the tools of his trade; at first, they feel blunt-edged. The scenery looks jerry-rigged; the dialect sounds mannered. Pete and Jimmie and the mother are monotonally strident, and the heroine's fate appears overordained. Melodrama is the mode. The simplicity of such lines as "The baby, Tommie, died . . . She and Jimmie lived" is all too rare. So there's no point in calling this a work of full artistic maturity; the author's trying on prose attitudes for size.

Some critics suggest he began composing *Maggie* while still an undergraduate at Syracuse; an early draft avoids the name "Maggie" and is simply titled "A Girl of the Streets." The added specificity of the proper noun lends substance to the portrait, putting flesh on abstract bones. As *tract,* moreover, the text is effective, and its unsparing depiction of the downward spiral of sexual degradation must have been revelatory to his readership. Mary Helen Peck Crane's temperance lectures find dramatic expression here as well; the boozers and the brawlers are figures from the pulpit if not stage. The urban environment acts as a principal player,

and a maleficent one. It seems the writer witnessed children playing "King of the Castle" together—but pelting one another with
rocks, not snowballs—and from this incident fashioned his tale
"of the streets."

In 1893, at twenty-one, Crane published *Maggie* privately, with
a small inheritance from his mother, and under the pseudonym
of "Johnston Smith." It was not a commercial success. Here's an
inscription he wrote to Hamlin Garland in the first edition; very
similar ones were sent to others, and they signal his authorial purpose:

> It is inevitable that you be greatly shocked by this book but con-
> tinue, please, with all possible courage, to the end. For it tries to
> show that environment is a tremendous thing in the world and
> frequently shapes lives regardless. If one proves that theory, one
> makes room in Heaven for all sorts of souls (notably an occa-
> sional street girl) who are not confidently expected to be there
> by many excellent people. It is probable that the reader of this
> small thing may consider the Author to be a bad man, but, obvi-
> ously, that is a matter of small consequence to the Author

He would continue in this muckraking vein, writing stories
such as "A Great Mistake" and "An Ominous Baby" (based upon
the dead infant Tommie of the previous book) that limned lives
of the downtrodden poor. *George's Mother*, a kind of sequel to
*Maggie*, was similar in aspiration, though he put it aside to work
on a very separate sort of fiction—one set in the historical past.
In his book about the Civil War, Crane projects and does not describe experience; the great strength of *The Red Badge of Courage*
(1895) consists of his imaginative entry into a mind and body not

his own. The same held true for *Maggie*, of course, but there was a certain dispassion involved, as if he found a subject, then determined to treat it in prose. The first book feels programmatic in a way that this next one does not; the novelist enters a landscape—and describes it vividly—that had fired his imagination almost since the start.

Possibly apocryphal, but nonetheless telling, is an anecdote about a young drama critic, Acton Davies, who gave Crane a translation of Émile Zola's *La Débâcle*. When Crane dismissed the book, Davies—who admired Zola—was himself dismissive. This suggests his new ambition:

> "I suppose you could have done it better?"
> "Certainly," said Crane.

• • •

At twenty-three, more as an act of speculation than witness, he produced the seminal *The Red Badge of Courage*. There was a good deal of research involved; Crane got the details of the Battle of Chancellorsville almost entirely right. He visited the fields of Fredericksburg, Virginia, and read *Battles and Leaders of the Civil War*, a four-volume series of articles that had appeared in the *Century Illustrated Magazine* and were collectively published in 1888. Yet his first two novels should be read as a construction of previously imagined worlds; the cart precedes the horse. Crane's real familiarity with the Bowery came chronologically subsequent to his description thereof; he had not seen a battle until *Badge* established his credentials as a war correspondent. This too is an aspect of "the art of youth"; the untried soldier Henry Fleming is an alter ego, possibly, but not a nom de plume. The book is first and foremost a process of invention, and consciously bookish as well. Allusions to and echoes of antiquity are present everywhere. It's not merely Henry Fleming who dreams of ancient and epic encounters; his creator does so too.

Though the language strives for realism, and the dominant genre remains that of Naturalism, this is in central ways a tale told via archetype—more akin to Arthurian legend than, say, the wartime narratives of Norman Mailer or James Jones. "The tattered soldier," "the tall soldier," "the loud soldier," and so forth are representative figures rather more than individuals; we're in the world of symbolic action and tableau. The dead and dying soldiers partake of a kind of marmoreal stillness, and the movement of the armies is fixed as on a frieze. He had been reading Homer, then Zola and Guy de Maupassant and Tolstoy—who also wrote of battles that transpired long before, but who had known combat firsthand. Crane's novel, with its vivid opening passage ("The cold passed reluctantly from the earth, and the retiring fogs revealed an army stretched out on the hills, resting"), is *written*, line by page. By the second sentence ("As the landscape changed from brown to green, the army awakened, and began to tremble with eagerness at the noise of rumors"), we know we're in the realm of metaphoric as well as literal description. Personification abounds.

This is fiction of a higher order than *Maggie: A Girl of the Streets*. Although there are battles aplenty, the main action is internal; the young soldier's fears are spelled out with clinical precision. The dialogue persuades. And the rite of passage here depicted is near-universal: the "blooding" and maturation of a frightened boy. It's tempting to construe Henry Fleming's ruminations as to his own behavior in combat (his anxious self-examination as to whether he would run under fire) as autobiographical in essence, though not of course couched as memoir.

By comparison with *Maggie*, *An Episode of the American Civil War* (the novel's subtitle) is a detailed study. Though this book too is brief, it feels in no way hurried. Here are Fleming's first considerations:

> The youth . . . had, of course, dreamed of battles all his life — of vague and bloody conflicts that had thrilled him with their sweep and fire. In visions he had seen himself in many struggles. He had imagined peoples secure in the shadow of his eagle-eyed prowess. But awake he had regarded battles as crimson blotches on the pages of the past. He had put them as things of the bygone with his thought-images of heavy crowns and high castles. There was a portion of the world's history which he had regarded as the time of wars, but it, he thought, had been long gone over the horizon and had disappeared forever.
>
> From his home his youthful eyes had looked upon the war in his own country with distrust. It must be some sort of a play affair. He had long despaired of witnessing a Greeklike struggle. Such would be no more, he had said. Men were better, or more timid. Secular and religious education had effaced the throat-grappling instinct, or else firm finance held in check the passions.

· · ·

Now more than a century later, this book about the Civil War is still a must-read for high school students, and a canonical text. It brought Crane enduring fame and at least momentary fortune — though his prowess at spending outstripped his earning powers, and he was always in debt. *The Red Badge of Courage* remains his signature achievement, and if a reading audience knows nothing else about this writer, it will know about his novel; together with such titles as *Moby-Dick* and *Huckleberry Finn* it sits stage center on any shelf of American literature, and has kept its place.

Others have critiqued the work at length. What I want here to emphasize is how, at twenty-three, he managed to construct a word-world both private and public — how he tapped into and helped enlarge a nation's fascination with its storied past. Since Henry Fleming's history is imagined, not remembered, that "storied past" invents itself as an act of mythopoesis. (Consider, for a moment, the other two novels cited above; both *Moby-Dick* and *Huckleberry Finn* derive from firsthand knowledge of the places and action described.) But such figures as the corpse propped up against a tree, or the tall soldier doing his death-dance while his friends stand helplessly watching and such phrases as "The red sun was pasted in the sky like a wafer" — these are indelible. By the time "the youth" emerges as a full-fledged and seasoned warrior, the writer too has attained maturity. As the flag bearer in what becomes a victorious skirmish, Henry Fleming can report about his comrades: "The impetus of enthusiasm was theirs again. They gazed about them with looks of uplifted pride, feeling new trust in the grim, always confident weapons in their hands. And they were men."

Hamlin Garland and others have described a facility in composition that bordered on automatic writing. Joseph Conrad remembers that, when they shared a writing space, "for two hours or so not a sound would be heard in that room. At the end of that time

Crane would say suddenly: 'I won't do any more now, Joseph.' He would have covered three of his large sheets with his regular, legible, perfectly controlled, handwriting, with no more than half a dozen erasures—mostly single words—in the whole lot. It seemed to me always a perfect miracle in the way of mastery over material and expression."

Crane would enter a room and claim to have a poem in his head, then sit and transcribe without pause. The manuscripts document this; the image of artist as *vates* (possessed, hearing words in the echo chamber of his skull) does not encourage revision. Some considered it playacting, as if he'd memorized his lines and sat down to transcribe them in order to impress his audience. Some called it self-indulgence, others a heedless squandering of talent. Those with the advantage of hindsight were inclined to call it prophecy, as though Crane was sure of his imminent doom. He told Nellie Crouse he did not care to live past thirty-five; he subtracted four years from that total for Karl Harriman, and the phrase in which he called himself "a dry twig on the edge of the bonfire" suggests the vision of his own impending end. In a later short story, "The Veteran" (1896), as if to dispel any lingering question as to Henry Fleming's nature—whether a weakling or hero—Crane gives us "the youth" of The Red Badge of Courage when grown elderly. He is now a grandfather and admired by all; he cheerfully confesses that he knew cowardice in the early action at Chancellorsville. But he alone keeps his presence of mind while a barn burns, rescuing the animals. And he chooses to return for "two colts in the box-stalls at the back of the barn," though "it's sure death." The barn becomes a crucible—and death, apotheosis:

When the roof fell in, a great funnel of smoke swarmed to-
wards the sky, as if the old man's mighty spirit, released from
its body—a little bottle—had swelled like the genie of fable.
The smoke was tinted rose-hue from the flames, and perhaps
the unutterable midnights of the universe will have no power
to daunt the color of this soul.

. . .

In 1895, the year of *The Red Badge of Courage,* Crane also published *The Black Riders,* a book of poetry. One has the sense that,
throughout his career, he turned to verse for self-expression, and
in the traditional manner. Yet if he did so for traditional reasons,
his poetry seems anything but standard-issue rhyming; there's an
urgency, a directness of expression, that derives from Naturalism
and the "American Plain Style." Not for Crane the elaborate figure of speech or complicated formal structure; his pronounce-
ments have the feel of argumentative assertion as to the nature of
things. God and Truth and justice and injustice figure in the pages
repeatedly; the young writer grapples with large questions and
ideas about existence in little irregular lines. Disregard the bluster
and the posturing and you hear an original voice: a speaker wrestling with and then promulgating his opinions about faith and
love and disaster and death. These poems are—no better word
for it—odd.

Thomas Hardy at life's end was principally a poet, embrac-
ing the genre with which he had begun; at a certain point, and
for a multitude of reasons, he left prose fiction behind. But the
aging recluse did this in his final decades, working well into his
eighties, and it's hard to know if that pattern would have proved
the case for Crane. By comparison with his voluminous produc-

tion of journalism and prose fiction, his poetical output is scant. The poems themselves are most often short ones, rarely attaining the length of a sonnet and only very rarely extending to a second page. Again, he wrote at speed. Was poetry a "passing fancy," therefore, or might it have been central to Stephen Crane's achievement?

My own guess is the latter. His engagement with the genre seems somehow separate from his commitment to prose, whether in the creative or the journalistic mode. William Dean Howells introduced him to the poetry of Emily Dickinson, reading her work to him when they first met and establishing, if not influence, a sense of possibility. There's an elective affinity here: the same intensity, the same compressed expressiveness. Walt Whitman, with his discursive verse and experience of wartime, stands more plausibly as antecedent than "the belle of Amherst," but in his best poetic efforts Crane conjoins the two. The young artist did away, right from the start, with the formal exigencies of meter and rhyme; there's an immediacy to his writing—witness this chapter's epigraph and the five-line dialogue between "a man" and "the universe"—that argues a real fealty to verse. He thought of it as "the more ambitious effort"—treating "ideas of life as a whole." This revelatory letter was printed as "A Remarkable First Success" in *Demorest's Family Magazine* in May 1896:

I have heard a great deal about genius lately, but genius is a very vague word; and as far as I am concerned I do not think it has been rightly used. Whatever success I have had has been the result simply of imagination coupled with great application and concentration. It has been a theory of mine ever since I began to write, which was eight years ago, when I was sixteen, that the most artistic and the most enduring literature was that which reflected life accurately. Therefore I have tried to observe closely, and to set down what I have seen in the simplest and most concise way . . .

Personally, I like my little book of poems, "The Black Riders," better than I do "The Red Badge of Courage." The reason is, I suppose, that the former is the more ambitious effort. In it I aim to give my ideas of life as a whole, so far as I know it, and the latter is a mere episode,—an amplification. Now that I have reached the goal for which I have been working ever since I began to write, I suppose I ought to be contented; but I am not. I was happier in the old days when I was always dreaming of the thing I have now attained. I am disappointed with success. Like many things we strive for, it proves when obtained to be an empty and a fleeting joy.

There may be some false modesty in his closing declaration, but the assertions ring true. As Malcolm Lowry later would write, "Success is like some horrible disaster," and it's the case the unknown Stephen Crane seems more at ease in his skin than does the public figure. Whether success was truly a disappointment to the twenty-five-year-old is conjectural; he admits to having "reached the goal for which I have been working ever since I began to write." And it's the exceptional young artist who hopes to be ignored while "dreaming of" future fame. But the "empty and a fleeting joy" he reports on does feel accurate; no sooner did Crane find himself a center of attention than he did what he could to escape.

That escape took the form, once again, of journalism. *Red*

*Badge* was well and widely reviewed, and paid assignments ensued. Once a stringer for neighborhood newspapers, he became a full-fledged correspondent, traveling through the American West and then south to Mexico and sending back dispatches from the field. He wrote articles for various newspapers and magazines, producing them at a great rate and with mixed results. Sometimes he was hailed as an important innovator, sometimes dismissed as a fraud. There were panegyrics and outpourings of praise; there were insults too. Even "The Red Badge of Hysteria" came in for an assault. On April 11, 1896, Alexander C. McClurg—who did fight in the Civil War and mistakenly believed the novel to have been published first in England—sent an outraged letter to the *Dial:*

> Under such circumstances we cannot doubt that "The Red Badge of Courage" would be just such a book as the English would grow enthusiastic over, and we cannot wonder that the redoubtable "Saturday Review" greeted it with the highest encomiums, and declared it to be the actual experiences of a veteran of our War, when it was really the vain imaginings of a young man born long since that war, a piece of intended realism based entirely on unreality. The book is a vicious satire upon American soldiers and American armies . . .

Crane took such criticism, it appears, in stride. If thin-skinned, he did not display it—though sometimes, for the sake of anonymity, he assumed an alias while preparing a newspaper story. He inscribed a copy of *The Third Violet* to Frank Harris (the influential editor of the *Fortnightly*):

Dear Mr. Harris.
   This book is even worse than any of the others.
Stephen Crane
London, June, 1897

This tongue-in-cheek self-deprecation would stay with him, and it was part of his charm. In his dedications, often, he dismissed the text at hand. More and more the man behaved as might a grizzled veteran, recalling that blond boy who walked into a river without knowing how to swim. If Edgar Allan Poe preceded him (there's a distant physical resemblance, as well as a shared fascination with catastrophe), Ernest Hemingway would follow. Hemingway patterned his own career—as cub reporter, short story writer, war correspondent, novelist—in large part on Stephen Crane's. The model of artist as reporter-adventurer was one the young Midwesterner would take to heart a generation later; his motto of "grace under pressure" applies in retrospect. An older Hemingway would claim to have liberated Paris in World War II, drinking champagne in the cafés while General Leclerc and the regular troops advanced. Crane, earlier, did the actual thing; in Puerto Rico he walked alone into the village of Juana Diaz. According to Richard Harding Davis (writing in *Harper's* magazine in May of 1899), "his khaki suit, slouched hat and leggings were all that was needed to drive the first man he saw, or rather the man who first saw him, back upon the town in disorderly retreat . . ."

So by the time the troops arrived, the correspondent had taken the field. His heroism under fire, his endurance when shipwrecked, his drinking bouts and whoring and all-night poker games—these were part of young Crane's legend and his behavioral mode. But always there's the sense of ironical self-imposed distance as well: a man who strikes a pose in order to gauge its effect. It is as though he felt himself, the watcher, watched.

For there were many who did. Here's one later critic's assessment:

> Certainly, early fame probably did Stephen Crane more harm than good. The brilliant achievement of *The Red Badge of Courage,* published when Crane was just twenty-three years old, an achievement that was so obvious that even mediocre critics recognized that Crane had a unique genius, and an achievement that made Crane an overnight literary celebrity, created critical and public expectations that thereafter caused Crane to squander his genius and destroy his health while trying to live up to his reputation as a man who could capture the true essence of war.

Philip Holthaus goes on to argue that Crane wasted his talent by finding it imperative to report on actual, rather than imagined, war; his time spent as a reporter in the Southwest and Mexico, then as a war correspondent (in Cuba in 1896, Greece the next year during the Greco-Turkish War, and Cuba once more in the Spanish-American War) did little to advance his art. But Holthaus's first sentence, with its contradictory adverbs, "certainly" and "probably," puts the issue in fuzzed, if no doubt inadvertent, focus; we cannot know what might have happened had Crane remained at his desk. "The Open Boat" would not have found its narrative occasion had he not been reporting on an actual harrowing trip. It's impossible to know — and this is true in general of "the art of youth" — what more might have ensued. To ask what else Crane might have done is to receive no answer. The only certainty is that his time was truncated and his career as artist proved lamentably brief.

Joseph Conrad writes about Crane feelingly, twenty years after the loss of his friend:

> Many people imagined him a fiery individuality. Certainly he was not cold-blooded. But his was an equable glow, morally and temperamentally. I would have said the same of his creative power (I have seen him sit down before a blank sheet of paper, dip his pen, write the first line at once and go on without haste and without pause for a couple of hours), had he not confided to me that his mentality did flag at times. I do not think it was anything more than every writer is familiar with at times. Another man would have talked of his 'failing inspiration.' It is very characteristic of Crane that I have never heard him use that word when talking about his work.

Ford Madox Ford memorializes him fondly as well:

> Crane was the most beautiful spirit I have ever known. He was small, frail, energetic, at times virulent. He was full of fantasies and fantasticisms. He would fly at and deny every statement before it was out of your mouth. He wore breeches, riding leggings, spurs, a cowboy's shirt and there was always a gun near him in the medieaval building that he inhabited seven miles from Winchelsea. In that ancient edifice he would swat flies with precision and satisfaction with the bead-sight of his gun . . .

And Henry James, two days after Crane's death, would write of his compatriot:

> What a brutal needless extinction—what an unmitigated unredeemed catastrophe! I think of him with such a sense of possibilities & powers.

• • •

But there are many dark-eyed men foredoomed to early death who do not leave important books upon a shelf. Why we remember Crane at all has less to do with derring-do than with his canonical novel, his poetry and tales. He wrote only sparingly about the act of writing, and his literary criticism is next to nonexistent. He claimed not to be "carnivorous" about the work of his contemporaries, and he was self-taught. So it's difficult to know if he himself distinguished between fool's gold and the rare metal of his best short stories—if, I mean, he understood why "The Bride Comes to Yellow Sky" was worth ten of her bridesmaids or "The Blue Hotel" was an enduring edifice, not a pup tent pitched on sand. And—to pursue Ford Madox Ford's description—there was something scattershot about Crane's marksmanship. To "swat flies . . . with the bead-sight of his gun" is to demonstrate agility but hit no serious target; the best sits catercorner to the worst.

(This is true, not incidentally, of Ford as well; that the author of *The Good Soldier* and *Parade's End* should also have produced such novels as *When the Wicked Man* and *Ladies Whose Bright Eyes* suggests a kind of doubling, as though the left hand went on scribbling while the right hand took a rest. Years later, Graham Greene would engage in similar bifurcation—labeling some of his books "entertainment" while others require close scrutiny. Not every artist follows the Joycean model of repeated — even obsessive — revision or the high ideal of excellence in every published text. "Hackwork" need not be only a pejorative term, and the voluminous productions of Sir Walter Scott and Anthony Trollope necessarily include some second-rank writing as well. When Dr. Johnson asserted that "no man but a blockhead ever wrote, except for money," he was stating a position to which Crane would adhere.)

But from the moment we read, "None of them knew the color of the sky" — the first line of "The Open Boat" — we know we're in the presence of an artist at work at the top of his bent. This tale of stress and survival is as central to the oeuvre as *The Red Badge of Courage;* it also was composed at speed but with the feel of an action rehearsed. Crane reported on the real shipwreck a few days after the event for the *New York Press* (which gave it the heading "Stephen Crane's Own Story"), and only six months later did the fictionalized version appear in *Scribner's Magazine.* Here for the first time Crane was writing (as autobiographer, not journalist) of something he'd witnessed firsthand; he had relied before on research and imagination, but now his verbal prowess and psychological acuity were pressed into the service of personal account. The subtitle of the story — "A Tale Intended to be after the Fact: Being the Experience of Four Men From the Sunk Steamer *Commodore*" — reports on that ill-fated trip; the experience described is that of a collective effort. We can distinguish between them (both visually and verbally), but the four sailors function as one.

The SS *Commodore* set out from Jacksonville, Florida, one of three "filibustering" vessels carrying men and munitions to the Cuban rebels. Crane secured passage aboard. A few hours out of port, there was a mysterious explosion—caused, perhaps, by sabotage—in the boiler room. The steamship foundered, then sank. Together with the captain and two members of the crew, the writer battled heavy seas for almost thirty hours in a ten-foot dinghy. They rowed and rowed toward the shore, eventually capsizing in surf off Daytona Beach. "The Open Boat" is his account of that harrowing experience and—by the attestation of others who survived it—accurate.

The "correspondent" reports on his adventure with the cook, the oiler, and the captain; there's a good deal of dialogue, a good deal of it humorous, and the conversations ring true. Crane's recurrent subject—the interaction of human nature with an indifferent natural world—is explored throughout in balanced cadences: "Slowly and beautifully the land loomed out of the sea. The wind came again. It had veered from the northeast to the southeast. Finally a new sound struck the ears of the men in the boat. It was the low thunder of the surf on the shore." The narrative style displays once more his characteristic dispassion and ironical stance. Yet though the whole consists of past-tense presentation, since the tale is "Intended to be after the Fact," there's an immediacy to the telling that offers up emotion not recollected in tranquility but raw.

Early on we read that "the correspondent, pulling at the other oar, watched the waves and wondered why he was there." By story's end, we know. And though "it would be difficult to describe the subtle brotherhood of men that was here established on the seas," Crane does so admirably. The men had neither slept nor eaten much the night before; they are inexpert rowers and swim-mers; they urge one another on. All four of them are subject to hazard—in the case of the oiler, fatal. After the dinghy flings them free and they try to swim ashore, we read a scene of incom-parable efficiency. These lines come from the point of view of the correspondent as a rescue party nears:

> Then he saw the man who had been running and undressing, and undressing and running, come bounding into the water. He dragged ashore the cook, and then waded toward the captain, but the captain waved him away and sent him to the correspon-dent. He was naked—naked as a tree in winter, but a halo was about his head, and he shone like a saint. He gave a strong pull, and a long drag, and a bully heave of the correspondent's hand. The correspondent, schooled in the minor formulae, said, "Thanks, old man." But suddenly the man cried, "What's that?" He pointed a swift finger. The correspondent said, "Go."
>
> In the shallows, face downward, lay the oiler. His forehead touched sand that was periodically, between each wave, clear of the sea . . .
>
> The welcome of the land to the men from the sea was warm and generous; but a still and dripping shape was carried slowly up the beach, and the land's welcome for it could only be the different and sinister hospitality of the grave.

This could not be better done. There's the vision of the naked rescuer who "shone like a saint," the behavior of the captain who waves off assistance and sends help to others, the "correspondent, schooled in the minor formulae," who reveals his social class with "Thanks, old man." There's the quick dialogue between them, the sudden shocking image of the oiler on the sand, and the austere evocation of the "still and dripping shape." "The Open Boat" is both brief and expansive, a work of mastered craft.

The same holds true—to a lesser extent—for other examples of his short fiction. "The Bride Comes to Yellow Sky" (1898) and "The Blue Hotel" (1899) are written by a man at ease with the techniques of narration. Both stories are action-packed and cinematic in their structure: scene hurtles after scene. Here Crane is not so much a witnessing presence as a yarn spinner; his crew of drinkers and cowards and braggarts could well step onto the screen of early Westerns to come. The sheriff and his bride in "Yellow Sky," the gambler and the Swede in "The Blue Hotel," are representative figures in the mode of "the youth" and "the tall soldier" from *The Red Badge of Courage*. "The Knife," "His New Mittens," and "The Price of the Harness" belong in that company too.

In these latter instances, however, we're in the world of central casting rather more than allegory. The landscape is a painted backdrop, with dust and blazing sunshine and saloon doors and cowboys brawling behind them, then drunks brandishing guns or gamblers wielding knives to sudden and lethal effect. These stories antedate the advent of the motion picture and, thereafter, television. But the author's imagination seems, essentially, that of the screenplay or TV sitcom writer. My assumption is that, had he lived today, Crane would have sought to swell his bank account by writing for contemporary media. He would have welcomed a microphone and camera, leaving prose fiction behind. As a journalist, he would have blogged. From time to time he dabbled in the theater, though with no commercial success; one project (which he proposed to Joseph Conrad) was to mount a Western in the West End. There was to be a climactic chase scene, with young lovers in a canyon and two dead horses on the stage; it failed for want of props.

His most ambitious effort, the novella-length "The Monster," also partakes of a precinematic strategy. This story is not so much written as shown, and he's back to the kind of presentational prose that structured *Maggie: A Girl of the Streets*. I mean by this that language is less crucial here than plot point or confrontation; what matters to the writer is the tale told and society revealed. Even a line such as "The doctor was shaving this lawn as if it were a priest's chin" is in essence visual, if not cinematic, and the image of a badly burned and monstrous Henry Johnson seems tailor-made for the screen. This parable of small-town small-mindedness is heavy-handed, admittedly, but here again its author casts his lot with the downtrodden of the earth. Crane's artistic claim to fame won't rest on these short narratives, but there's assurance to them, and a prodigious productivity in the final years.

He had several romantic attachments. One of his friends at Claverack, Armistead Borland, remembered the smooth moves of "Steve . . . my hero and ideal . . . I tried to copy him in every way and learned many things, not all for the good of my immortal soul—the rudiments of the great American game of poker and something more than the rudiments of the ways of a man with a maid." Although part of this is schoolboy braggadocio, it's clear that Crane pursued the company of women from the start.

There was a series of idealized damsels—Lily Brandon and Nellie Crouse principal among them—and no doubt a series of one-night stands, most of them for hire. He wrote ardent letters to a chorus line of ladies and styled himself a man familiar with the demimonde. In a letter to a friend of his who lived in Norfolk, Virginia, he wrote (on February 16, 1892, when not yet twenty-one):

> So you lack females of the white persuasion, do you? How unfortunate! And how extraordinary! I never thought that the world could come to such a pass that you would lack females, Thomas! You indeed must be in a God forsaken country. Just read these next few lines in a whisper: I—I think black is good good—if—if its [sic] yellow and young.

By contrast, he could write as well in the tones of mournful ardor, as when he complained (in the winter of 1893) to the now-married Lily Brandon Munroe:

> Your face is a torturous thing, appearing to me always, with the lines and the smile that I love—before me always this indelible picture of you with it's [sic] fragrance of past joys and it's [sic] persistent utterance of the present griefs which are to me tragic, because they say they are engraven for life. It is beyond me to free myself from the thrall of my love for you; it comes always between me and what I would enjoy in life—always—like an ominous sentence—the words of the parrot on the death-ship: "We are all damned."

And in the last of his series of letters to the thoroughly conventional Nellie Crouse, when she announced her engagement to another man, Crane wrote (on March 18, 1896):

Really, by this time I should have recovered enough to be able to write you a sane letter, but I cannot—my pen is dead. I am simply a man struggling with a life that is no more than a mouthful of dust to him.

· · ·

By the end of that year, however, the "mouthful of dust" would have changed its savor, and passion would be real. In an inscription from December 1896 to C.E.S., "an unnamed sweetheart" in Jacksonville, Florida, Crane writes:

> Brevity is an element
> That enters importantly
> Into all pleasures of
> Life, and this is what
> Makes pleasure sad
> And so there is no
> Pleasure but only sadness.

· · ·

The initials of the "unnamed sweetheart" C.E.S. stand for Cora Ethel Stewart. Brevity, pleasure, and sadness all enter into this narrative; it structures Crane's last years. The hero and the heroine are in some ways star-crossed lovers, in other ways a mismatched and even comic pair. For the final period of his productive life, the young man from New Jersey lived in Sussex, England, in a crumbling baronial structure called Brede Place. There he and Cora Stewart played at keeping house. The writer introduced the lady to his newfound neighbors as "Mrs. Crane," but had met her a short while before as the proprietor of an establishment in Jacksonville, the Hotel de Dream.

Not technically a brothel because its clientele had to complete their transactions elsewhere, Hotel de Dream nonetheless served as a clearinghouse for assignations. Its owner, Ethel Dreme, sold this "hotel" to the Boston-born Cora, who in her early thirties would make of it a profitable enterprise. Previously, with her first husband, Thomas Vinton Murphy—the son of the former Collector of the Port of New York—she had also been engaged in business: running, it was rumored, munitions as well as a gambling house.

Once divorced, she married Captain Donald William Stewart, a minor member of the British upper classes who served in India, then Africa in the war against the Ashanti. Cora refused to accompany him on his military missions and embarked instead, in England, on a series of very public affairs. Stewart was jealous and unforgiving (though not, apparently, as jealous as would be a later consort, Hammond P. McNeill, who shot and killed one of her lovers after Crane himself was dead). The woman oscillated wildly—as did her writer-companion—between respectability and recklessness; in the end, as Cora Taylor, she would return to Jacksonville and operate a full-fledged whorehouse called the Court as well as a tropical bordello called the Palmetto Lodge.

Nomenclature matters. She was born Cora Ethel Eaton Howarth, of refined parentage in Massachusetts. Then she married, in succession, Messrs. Murphy, Stewart, McNeill, and a Colonel Taylor—not all of them, apparently, after the wearisome legalities of previous divorce. Her marriage to McNeill was almost certainly bigamous; she never married Crane. Mrs. Stephen Crane (let's call her by that name, since it's the one with which she signed her letters) is a complicated figure: prosperous by birth and elegant to start with, then blowsy and impoverished and fierce. She is reputed to have flung herself overboard from a yacht, clad only in a nightgown, in order to swim to the safety of shore when fleeing an abusive lover; she was Crane's fellow traveler in the war in Greece and Turkey, earning the title of war correspondent at least as bravely as did he. And though she caused such men as Henry James discomfiture by her "irregular" alliance with the dying artist, she does seem to have cared for him with passionate concern. Cora cast her lot with the young writer for many reasons surely: his fame, his generous spirit, the company he kept. But judging by the letters with which she asked his friends and relatives for help, then the accents of real grief with which she described his failing health and final days, she did so also for love.

Although we have no detailed record of their early meetings, it's clear the two adventurers were kindred from the start. And while they behaved like kindred spirits, the photographs suggest as well that opposites attract. Where the man is lean, dark-haired, and pallid, the woman is, as the euphemism goes, full-figured: light-complexioned and robust. They are Jack and Mrs. Sprat. To see Cora in working regalia in the uniform of a war correspondent, with a canteen slung across her chest (a photo taken in Athens, in 1897) is to see a formidable person, and not one to be trifled with; batted eyelashes and modest downward glances form no part of her style.

Stephen and Cora met in Jacksonville while he was en route to Cuba, and where he frequented brothels. Whether he first paid for her company we are unlikely to know. But they bonded rapidly (as the dedication above makes clear) while the correspondent sought the wherewithal to travel on. We have no record, either, of their parting words and intentions; perhaps his claim that "brevity is an element" of the pleasures of life was his way of saying good-bye. Four days later, however—although this was of course not part of their plan—he returned. The SS *Commodore* sank. After the misadventure of shipwreck recorded in "The Open Boat," he wired Cora for money and help, and she traveled to Daytona Beach and brought him back to Jacksonville. There he convalesced.

The front-page news of the *Commodore* disaster and his bravery when shipwrecked did much to restore Crane's public image (one that had been tarnished by his defense of a prostitute in the Manhattan courts; he claimed she had been wrongly arrested by the police, and was lampooned for having confused a scarlet letter and red badge). When the writer had regained his strength, if not his health altogether, he tried to return to Cuba via a trip to New York, but a blockade had been established and he chose another conflict to report on. Crane signed with William Randolph Hearst's *New York Journal,* to cover the impending Greco-Turkish War; Cora sold Hotel de Dream and—without a backward glance, it seems—left America as well.

As correspondents they were busy and productive. They traveled to London, then Marseille and Athens; he wrote dispatches on the Greek war for the McClure syndicate, and Cora, writing under the byline "Imogene Carter," described "War Seen Through a Woman's Eyes"—one of the first such perspectives—for the *New York Journal.* From Athens they traveled to Thessaly and the small town of Velestino, where a battle raged. On the battlefield Crane found and saved a puppy, which was stolen from him at Volos and recovered again at Chalcis, to which they fled by ship. His description of the evacuation of Volos, sent from Chalcis, appeared under the headline "The Blue Badge of Cowardice" in Hearst's newspaper, and Cora too reported feelingly about the Greek withdrawal. Both of them were energized by the conflict they observed.

There followed a brief period while they tried to decide where to settle; in England, Crane composed his novella, "The Monster," and some of his best short stories, including "The Bride Comes to Yellow Sky," "Death and the Child," and "The Blue Hotel." *The Open Boat and Other Tales of Adventure* appeared in April 1898. Then Crane set sail once more, traveling to Cuba and producing a set of dispatches from Havana and writing many of the war stories in the posthumously published *Wounds in the Rain* (1900). This trip was undertaken without Cora, and his increasing distance and extended silence made her frantic; to Arnold Bennett, for instance, she wrote on 3 September, 1898:

> Stephen was sent from Cuba to Hampton Roads on an army transport as a typhoid suspect. Then he felt obliged to go to Porto [sic] Rico and is now said to be in Havana. If you have a line from him please let me know instantly. His family can not give me an address. I am so anxious.

He did return, however, and they settled down. His health grew worse. As always, ceaselessly, he smoked. Witness after witness describes him as pale, rail-thin, and consumptive (explaining, perhaps, the suspicion of typhoid) and beginning to cough blood. Nonetheless, the couple established themselves, first in a plain brick structure called Ravensbrook in Oxted, and then in the rambling manor house in Sussex. Here they chose to live in part because of the proximity to writers such as Joseph Conrad, Ford Madox Ford, Harold Frederic, Henry James, and H. G. Wells, a community of artists that meant much to Crane. His friendship with Conrad in particular was immediate and warm. From Moreton Frewen, a wealthy dilettante, the pair leased Brede Place cheaply, with a promise they proved unable to keep of maintaining and improving the property. What follows is a description of the building, taken from an architectural survey of the region; it must have pleased the Americans mightily to camp in so ancient a structure, with its fabled ghosts:

> The earlier part of the house was built by Sir Thomas Oxenbridge, who died November 1497, and Sir Goddard, who died in February 1531 . . . The house is strangely ill-arranged internally. The hall, which once rose to the whole height of the building, has been subdivided into an upper and lower floor . . . The Place was long a satisfactory resort of smugglers, as the legends attached to Sir Goddard kept people away, and counted to them for all the strange sounds which were heard there.
>
> *Groaning Bridge* is pointed out as the spot where Sir Goddard Oxenbridge was sawn in half by the children.

That passage comes from a contemporary guidebook; here's a personal remembrance of Brede Place offered by H. G. Wells in his *Experiment in Autobiography:*

> I remember very vividly a marvelous Christmas Party in which Jane and I participated. We were urged to come over and, in a postscript, to bring any bedding and blankets we

could spare. We arrived in a heaped-up Sandgate cab, rather in advance of the guests from London. We were given a room over the main gateway in which there was a portcullis and an owl's nest, but at least we got a room. Nobody else did—because although some thirty or forty invitations had been issued, there were not as a matter of fact more than three or four bedrooms available. One of them however was large and its normal furniture had been supplemented by a number of hired truckle-beds and christened the Girls' Dormitory, and in the attic an array of shake-downs was provided for the men. Husbands and wives were torn apart . . .

Anyhow there were good open fires in the great fireplaces and I remember that party as an extraordinary lark—but shot, at the close, with red intimations of a coming tragedy. We danced in the big oak-panelled room downstairs, lit by candles stuck upon iron sconces that Cora Crane had improvised with the help of the Brede blacksmith.

Unfortunately she had not improvised grease guards and after a time everybody's back showed a patch of composite candle-wax, like the flash on the coat of a Welsh Fusilier.

• • •

Once more it makes sense to consider Crane's youth. Lionized by twenty-five, he must have feared himself a cub; the heady admiration he received upon arrival in England (an arrival trumpeted by newspapers) could only have gone to his head. He embraced the role of country squire, riding out daily with his dogs; one has the sense that he engaged in dress-up at Brede Place. Those "red intimations of a coming tragedy" to which H. G. Wells alludes were hemorrhages. Though Crane grew protective of his privacy (withdrawing to the far corners of the estate and the cold heights of the building), that privacy proved unavailable. Guest after guest arrived. It's troubling to think of the young writer in an upstairs garret while a clutch of visitors clamored for attention in the public rooms below; he was paying the price of success.

Before he died, tubercular, in a spa in Germany, Crane seemed an emblem of the poète maudit, a blazing talent foredoomed by disease to premature collapse. To borrow a phrase from "The Open Boat," the end of his life was "most wrongfully and barbarously abrupt." The extent to which willful self-destruction is implicit in such fascination with destruction is of course conjectural, but it surprised no one who knew him that Stephen Crane died young.

He was, to say the least, an indifferent steward of his own person; he ate too little, drank too much, slept sometimes not at all. And he was self-aware. In mid-August of 1899, he wrote to an unidentified correspondent: "Please have the kindness to keep your mouth shut about my health in front of Mrs. Crane hereafter. She can do nothing for me and I am too old to be nursed. It is all up with me but I will not have her scared. For some funny woman's reason she likes me. Mind this."

Modern medicine might plausibly have cured what killed him at the start of the twentieth century; the patient's life could well have been—with proper care—prolonged. Even then, consumption was not necessarily lethal. Robert Louis Stevenson, for example, died of something other than the tuberculosis with which he'd been diagnosed; in the wet heat of the South Seas he outlasted his doctors' prognosis. But caution and moderation never were part of Crane's style. Ford Madox Ford writes of his dying days:

The final tragedy of poor Stevie did not find him wanting. It was tragedy. The sunlight fell blighted into that hollow, the specters waved their draped arms of mist, the parasites howled and belched on the banks of Brede. That was horrible. But much more horrible was the sight of Crane at his labours. They took place in a room in the centre bar of the E of the Place, over the arched entry. Here Crane would sit writing, hour after hour and day after day, racked with the anxiety that he would not be able to keep going with his pen alone all that fantastic crew. His writing was tiny; he used great sheets of paper. To see him begin at the top of the sheet with his tiny words was agonizing; to see him finish a page filled you with concern. It meant the beginning of one more page, and so till his death. Death came slowly, but Brede was a death-trap to the tuberculous.

Clearly, the climate and the lack of comforts at Brede Place were wrong for a man with his condition. And equally clearly he drove himself hard, at work until the end. Crane wrote *Active Service,* a novel that he himself described as "bad," in 1899; he wrote *Wounds in the Rain,* a collection of stories relating to the Spanish-American War; he further produced a series of articles on *Great Battles of the World.* These were published after his death, in 1900 and 1901 respectively. It's impossible to argue that *The Whilomville Stories* or *Last Words* — also posthumously published and products of the final period — were serious as works of art; he was writing to put loaves on the table, and doing so at speed.

Cora was complicit here, sending frantic letters to publishers and relatives, soliciting assistance (mostly fiscal), while admitting that Crane was unwell. To read her correspondence is to sense her desperation; their expenditures were large, their earnings small. And they seemed always in debt. In her manuscript book for December 1898, she wrote, "My letters are one long inky howl!" His parents might have called the comparison a blasphemy, but the image of crucifixion on a "real cross" of cash informs one of his last (unpublished) poems:

> My cross!
> Your cross?
> The real cross
> Is made of pounds,
> Dollars or francs.
> Here I bear my palms for the silly nails
> To teach the lack
> —The great pain of lack—
> Of coin.

The straw Crane grasped at in order to remedy the "lack of coin" was his novel in progress, *The O'Ruddy*. It occupied the writer for much of his last year. Earlier, he had referred to it as "The Irish Romance" and even "Romance" (the title of a future collaborative effort by Joseph Conrad and Ford Madox Ford); Cora so describes it in her letters to the agent James B. Pinker. Though it was to be a new departure, with his first use of the first-person narrator, what we have is a pastiche of legends attaching to Brede Place and the coastal region.

There's local Sussex color, a ghost or two, and the brio of the tone stands in impressive contrast to the dark circumstance of composition. Lines like the following—"But Paddy was an honest man, even if he did not know it" or "a lot of machinery so ingenious that it would require a great lack of knowledge to thoroughly understand it"—retain his ironical good humor. And since he was a born tale-teller, the adventures have narrative pace. The book itself feels like an act of brave denial, its gaiety a *danse macabre*. But it would stretch the point to say this novel registers an advance in creative innovation; once more he wrote for money, and once more in vain.

Robert Barr was the writer Cora selected at the end to complete *The O'Ruddy*. (She had attempted, and failed, to interest Rudyard Kipling in the project, then H. B. Marriott Watson took two days to tell her no, then A.E.W. Mason took the better part of two years.) Finally, Barr did finish the book, and it appeared with both authors' names on the title page in 1903. *The O'Ruddy* paid off some debts—to Pinker in particular—yet neither Crane's reputation, nor that of his collaborator, improved as a result. (Crane's own work amounts to a small percentage of the finished thing, so it's unkind to charge him with artistic as well as physical deterioration. But Mozart's unfinished requiem or Van Gogh's Saint-Rémy paintings—to take just two examples—belong to a different order of effort. *The O'Ruddy* was neither a summing up nor an elegiac farewell; it was a writer and his companion angling after contracts and clamoring for payment page by chapter.) No part of the novel suggests, as does his poetry, a clear-eyed grappling with mortality; the book was a commercial venture first and last.

Barr had read the manuscript in progress and, according to Cora, pronounced it as good as *The Three Musketeers* when he visited the dying man in Dover, at the Lord Warden Hotel. This was the place where Crane gathered his strength before a channel crossing and characteristically misguided attempt to find a cure abroad. On June 8, 1900, Barr wrote to a mutual friend, Karl Harriman:

> When your letter came I had just returned from Dover, where I stayed four days to see Crane off for the Black Forest. There was a thin thread of hope that he might recover, but to me he looked like a man already dead. When he spoke or rather whispered, there was all the accustomed humor in his sayings. I said to him that I would go over to the Schwarzwald in a few weeks, when he was getting better, and that we would take some convalescent rambles together. As his wife was listening he said faintly, "I'll look forward to that," but he smiled at me and winked slowly, as much as to say, "You damned humbug, you know I'll take no more rambles in this world."

Joseph Conrad reports on a visit to the Lord Warden as well. Fourteen years Crane's senior—and someone who did not put pen to paper till the age of twenty-eight—he writes in the accents of loss:

> I saw him for the last time on his last day in England. It was in Dover, in a big hotel, in a bedroom with a large window looking on the sea. He had been very ill and Mrs. Crane was taking him to some place in Germany, but one glance at that wasted face was enough to tell me that it was the most forlorn of all hopes. The last words he breathed out to me were: "I am tired. Give my love to your wife and child." When I stopped at the door for another look I saw that he had turned his head on the pillow and was staring wistfully out of the window at the sails

of a cutter yacht that glided slowly across the frame, like a dim shadow against the grey sky.

. . .

What finally are we to make of this astonishing artist, dead at twenty-eight? As he himself put it, "I have heard a great deal about genius lately, but genius is a very vague word . . . Whatever success I have had has been the result simply of imagination coupled with great application and concentration." The "imagination" is inarguable; he could conjure urban slums and battlefields based on short exposure and in persuasive detail. The "great application" is certain; the shelf of work belonging to Crane bulks easily as large as that produced by writers who lived twice as long. Yet "concentration" is less clear; much of what he wrote, it seems, was on automatic pilot and composed in haste. He was at best an inattentive caretaker of his own gift; the grain was always compromised by chaff. So it remains an open question if the word "genius" applies—though insofar as it entails a quicker ratio to the passage of time than that of ordinary mortals, the term is anything but "vague." The answer must be "yes."

Crane's worldly rise was explosive, his fall a sputtering out. Even now it's hard to credit that he died so soon and wrote so much. And since Stevie was always his own contradiction, his second act could have foundered on inconsequence or equally as plausibly have advanced his art. In my own perhaps wishful opinion, the latter is more probable. The men whose company he sought in England were committed to the dictates of craft; Conrad, Ford, and James would not have made him welcome in their circle had they believed him a trifler. Crane was a quick study, and an ambitious one; the collapse of his career is a function neither of insufficient talent nor insouciance but disease.

In an obituary notice written under one of her pseudonyms, "Henry Nickelman," Willa Cather recounts the following:

> Quite without invitation on my part, Crane began to talk, began to curse his trade from the first throb of creative desire in a boy to the finished work of the master . . . He gave me to understand that he led a double literary life, writing in the first place the matter that pleased himself, and doing it very slowly; in the second place, any sort of stuff that would sell. And he remarked that his poor was just as bad as it could possibly be.

Was his a talent wasted or fulfilled? That image of the artist bent to the desk in his garret at Brede, trying to complete a page while downstairs the creditors and partygoers gather, is somehow very modern—an emblem of focus as well as distraction. Celebrity is a double-edged sword; for Crane it cut both ways. He worked in a commercial trap of his own devising: self-invented, self-annulled.

During the five-year period before his death and after *The Red Badge of Courage,* Crane wrote near-ceaselessly. And though much of what he wrote was "just as bad as it could possibly be," he did from time to time produce "the matter that pleased himself." Although best known as a novelist (for his imaginative entry into the landscape of the Civil War) and journalist (for his coverage of wars in Greece and Turkey, his dispatches from Cuba, and the account of survival after shipwreck), the poetry of *War Is Kind* suggests a new direction and ambition. So do such stories as "The

Blue Hotel," "The Monster," and "The Bride Comes to Yellow Sky." Therefore the *what if* remains; certain passages are neither diminished nor spent.

A brief anguished poem seems apposite here:

Many red devils ran from my heart
And out upon the page.
They were so tiny
The pen could mash them.
And many struggled in the ink.
It was strange
To write in this red muck
Of things from my heart.

# 3

## *Dora Carrington*

I came to a great many agitating conclusions in the Louvre
this morning. A conflict always arises in reconciling my
passion for the early Sienese or the very early Florentine with
the amazing solidity of Titian and Giorgione. I tremble over
the delicate beauty of those little panels, the naïve simplicity
of their designs and the colour they are, but when I see
Titian and El Greco their powerful intellectual designs make
me stand still . . . When I am at the Louvre I suddenly feel
so certain of myself. I feel there is nothing to prevent my
painting my now fervent image of the nymph who turned
into a stag so perfectly that it could be no disgrace.

— DORA CARRINGTON, LETTER TO GERALD BRENAN, 1934

SHE LOOKS AT YOU; she is of course seeing herself. Your eyes
are the mirror she faces, though she does not confront her reflection directly, the eyes slanted up and away. Everything is slant-
ways in this pencil-on-paper self-portrait, the head of a girl not
quite woman, the way the face emerges from the left edge of the
page. The year is 1910. This is before she declared independence,

before she cut her hair. Carrington is seventeen. Her face looks much older, however, battered as though by a hard day's labor or a night's hard sleeplessness. The eye sockets are dark, deep. The pouches underneath her eyes look both a touch swollen and bruised; the suggestion of a tear appears on the left cheek. The nose is straight, lips full.

No vanity here, nor self-promotion in the time-honored modeling mode. She examines herself unblinkingly. Yet there's beauty in the image too; hers is an assessing glance you won't soon forget. The strokes are thick; the lead is blunt, the planes of the features established by juxtaposing white (the untouched portions of the sheet) and black. The light is less than flattering—cast by a candle or lantern, perhaps, and probably at nighttime and not in open air. Great skill in the handling of contrasts; some subtlety of modulation; the cross-hatching is assured. There's a certain weariness, a wariness, no hint of glad absorption in the task. Rather, this artist looks at her own limpid eyes and full-fleshed visage with the critical dispassion of a craftsperson devoted to craft.

It's now well past a century since Carrington drew this self-portrait, yet she seems wholly alive. As with any first-rate rendering in the realistic mode (particularly if there are no details specifying time and place), the dead become the quick. Hers is a masterly achievement for a draftsman still a teenager. Who drew this is a painter to watch watching; that upraised glance of hers haunts.

Dora Carrington was born more than twenty years after Stephen Crane, and she survived him by more than thirty. Her dates are 1893 to 1932. The two artists never met; it would have been surprising if they did. He died when she was young, of course, but there are additional reasons. If the writer was by temperament (though not in the end by circumstance) a solitary, the painter is associated with the company she kept—at first on the margins of and then closely linked to the group we label "Bloomsbury." If the former sent his work out unpolished and quickly, the latter was retentive. Where Crane rushed in heedless, she held herself back; where he found the limelight, she sought anonymity. It's hard to imagine them sharing a space: water adjacent to oil.

To the general public she stayed unknown. The first retrospective exhibition of Carrington's art was not held till 1970, in the Upper Grosvenor Galleries in London. (Nor should she be confused with the more celebrated and unrelated Leonora Carrington—whose work *is* widely represented on museum walls.) Still today, the bulk of her labor resides in private hands; her portraits of Lytton Strachey and of E. M. Forster—together with one or two landscapes—are her best-known paintings. It's difficult to guess what Carrington herself would make of her present recognition; her withdrawal from the world of gallery display was absolute. One has the sense that she recoiled from striving and careerism in an almost physical fashion; too, she had sufficient funding and did not need to sell. As the director of the Tate Gallery, Sir John Rothenstein, would write in 1976: "Her remoteness from the impulses which moved the most considerable of her contemporaries is at least one of the reasons why she has been the most neglected serious painter of her time."

Carrington was not, however, a person who could be ignored. Much photographed, she rarely looked at the camera head-on; self-critical, she proved far harder on herself than were her admirers. Men and women loved her; she seemed not to understand why. Her erotic life was beleaguered and confusing from the start. Part of the circumstance is personal; hers was a peculiar (and perhaps peculiarly British) amalgam of assertiveness and doubt. But part of it is surely also historical and cultural; at the start of the twentieth century it was unusual for female artists to be taken seriously, though Carrington was a star pupil at the prestigious Slade School of Fine Art. And when the other women of your circle include Vanessa Bell, Ottoline Morrell, Julia Strachey, and Virginia Woolf, the spotlight you shrink from will readily focus elsewhere.

Nonetheless the figure of Carrington served as the inspiration for a number of minor fictional characters. She was Minette Darrington in D. H. Lawrence's *Women In Love* and Mary Bracegirdle in Aldous Huxley's *Crome Yellow*, the doll-woman Betty Blyth in Wyndham Lewis's *The Apes of God* and the painter-photographer Anna Cory in Rosamond Lehmann's *The Weather in the Streets*.

If D. H. Lawrence disguised Carrington transparently as "Darrington," Emma Thompson brought her stage center in the movie *Carrington* (1995), written and directed by Christopher Hampton. That film focuses on the long and complex intimacy of its title character and the writer Lytton Strachey, as well as her romantic imbroglios with Mark Gertler, Ralph Partridge, Gerald Brenan, and others of the Bloomsbury set. She and Gertler were also the protagonists of a novel, *Mendel*, written by Gilbert Cannan; she makes cameo appearances in several other books. So the painter who determinedly kept her gaze averted from the camera has become a kind of icon of artistic sensibility—and all the more so because of how and why she died.

Her birthplace was in Hereford and she was raised in the provincial town of Bedford, not fifty miles from London—roughly the same distance as Brede Place. The most efficient description of their antecedents comes from her brother Noel:

> Dora Carrington, fourth child in a family of five, was born at Hereford in 1893. Her father, Samuel Carrington, son of a Liverpool merchant, had gone to India as a young man in 1857, the year of the Mutiny, to build railways for the East India Company. He did not retire until he was in his fifties and his letters to his parents over these many years have survived. They give a picture of a God-fearing man, devoted to his parents and a kind master to the Indians who worked under his charge. By the time he retired to England, after traveling through much of the East and in America, both his two sisters had long been married, each with a family of a dozen; so that his many nieces and nephews were already raising families in their turn. One of these nieces, Ethel, had married Frank Houghton, who had died in a yachting accident leaving her five children to bring up. Her sister-in-law, Charlotte Houghton, was thus brought into the Carrington circle and was acting as help or governess to the Houghton children when Samuel returned to England for good.

Samuel and Charlotte Houghton Carrington were married in 1888 and moved—with a frequency occasioned by her rheumatism and their attempt to find a moderate climate—to Hereford, then Somerset, Devon, Hampshire, Cheltenham, and, when daughter Dora was ten years old, to the town of Bedford. He had money and social position in the uneminent Victorian fashion: very much the proper (if slightly deaf) gentleman—pious and in later life invalided and benign. In part because he spent hours each day encased in a chair, he proved an excellent subject for portraiture; while she spent time with her father, she could, looking at him, draw. Carrington's oil portrait of the aging man is fond, evoking what she described as "his bright eyes and huge helpless body." He sits reading a newspaper, swaddled in blankets, unmoving. The face is small, the body large, the features precise, and the modeling deft. When he died at eighty-eight, she wrote: "I loved my father for his rough big character. His rustic simplicity and the great way he lived inside himself and never altered his life to please the conventions, or people of this century. He would have been exactly the same if he had lived under Elizabeth."

Her mother was, it would appear, the more conventional parent, and there's little registered warmth. Carrington complained of the woman's rigid religiosity; she made many sketches of her father and her brothers but no formal portrait of her mother, who was disinclined to sit. All discussion of bodily functions or sex was off-limits in the household; being pregnant was "being confined." The couple—a retired Indian Railways engineer married to an ex-governess—lived a life of stern propriety at 6 Rothsay Gardens, Bedford, and their daughter found it dull. Samuel seems to have encouraged her artistic aspirations, however, or at least not to have disapproved. Again, as Noel Carrington reports: "At no stage of her family life did Dora encounter opposition to her desire to be an artist. Her father liked to see his children using their hands and brains in leisure time. If Teddy could build model ships he was helped to get tools and timber, and if Dora loved to draw she was to have the materials."

Consistently, and starting at the age of twelve, she received awards judged by the Royal Drawing Society of Great Britain and Ireland. Young, she proved herself an accomplished draftsman and, from the outset, committed to color. The palette is, to start with, the standard English one: umber, sienna, bright oranges and reds, aquamarine, earth green. Her later life-studies of nudes, her portraits of local workers and friends, her village scenes and landscapes attest to her keen-sighted eye. The art mistress of the high school persuaded the family that Dora should attend art school — and at age seventeen she moved to London to do so, enrolling at the Slade School.

This was, for her, a providential escape; soon enough she left Bedford behind. By the end of the first year, "Carrington cropped her 'mother's glory' short enough to show the furrow in the nape of her neck; began to make her own unencumbered clothes; dropped her Christian name, which she considered vulgar and sentimental, and insisted on being known ever after as Carrington, *tout court*."

Her teachers — each of them a practicing artist — were Frederick Brown, Henry Tonks, and Philip Wilson Steer. Roger Fry was a visiting lecturer and Augustus John a reigning presence in the studio; these were inspiriting instructors, and she proved an apt pupil, progressing rapidly from copying out plaster casts of Michelangelo's *Dying Slave* and Greco-Roman sculpture to drawing nude models from life. She made female friends — finding kindred spirits at the Slade for the first time — and increasingly was noticed by the men. Young painters such as Mark Gertler, Paul Nash,

C.R.W. Nevinson, and Stanley Spencer were enrolled; Gertler fell for her heels over head. She was flattered by his attentions though, at eighteen, too young to reciprocate in physical terms, and the story of their relationship is not a happy one. As their exchange of letters suggests, her virginity was stonily defended, then yielded up with reluctance, and there was anger involved. *La vie passionnée* for Carrington was not a simple thing. But—to begin with, anyhow—her road to a career as artist seemed plausibly an open one, in spite of the veiled condescension attaching to "the fair sex." She had a great deal of talent and she showed it blazingly; by the end of her second year she received the much-coveted Slade scholarship, allowing her to continue her studies; by 1913 she won first prize both for Figure Painting and for Painting from the Cast. As Sir John Rothenstein observes: "She had another advantage, precocity. Had she not reached maturity so early, she might, again owing to her circumstances, have been prevented for all her innate talent from ever reaching it at all."

He means by this that, otherwise, Carrington would—*should,* by the standards of the period—have married and had children and withdrawn more or less modestly from the profession of art. "Copying" was part of her apprenticeship; the Slade instructed its students in the work of Sassetta and Giotto, Titian, Tintoretto, and the rest. Under the tutelage of Roger Fry, she came to admire the Impressionists and Post-Impressionists, most particularly Cézanne. Her enthusiasms ranged from Greek vases to Aubrey Beardsley, from Manet and Matisse to William Blake. Early on, she worked on frescoes; later she involved herself with the "decorative" arts. Carrington festooned her letters and diary pages with a kind of inspired doodling, her pencil rarely at rest. Like others of her circle, she painted walls and furniture and signs for shops and cabinets and floors. She designed the cover for *Two Stories,* the very first publication of Leonard and Virginia Woolf's new Hogarth Press. (It's worth noticing here that Virginia commissioned Carrington—and not her own sister Vanessa—to make those debut prints.) She cut woodblocks as well for such publications from Omega Press as *Simpson's Choice* (1915) and *Lucretius on Death* (1917). Her tiles for a fireplace, illustrations for books, decorated bureaus and caricatures and designs on glass could have been part and parcel of a young lady's attainment, the sort of amateur skill set expected of a wife. Mark Gertler urged her to learn how to cook; nonetheless she continued to paint.

Roughly fifty of her paintings have survived. Her letters and the diaries refer to many more. Some might be lost, or yet to surface, and some were no doubt destroyed. To begin with, this may have been a function of need; an impoverished young artist would simply paint over a canvas in order to save on the cost of material and begin again. For her first years in London, Carrington was poor. But later, with an inheritance from her supportive father, she would not have needed to economize and could have retained her paintings or stored them for future display. Instead, her dissatisfaction with the quality of her own efforts appears to have increased. The majority of canvases were made not as portraits for hire, or still lifes and landscapes produced in anticipation of a sale. She gave most of her labor away. But an industrious person working steadily for twenty years is likely to have produced much more; her cumulative output seems distressingly self-censored.

For this particular painter, the best was the enemy of the better and — unlike Stephen Crane, who sold and published whatever he could — she did not show a canvas until certain of its worth. When her friends from Slade began to exhibit and urged her to do the same with her work, Carrington held back; there was an exactingness and diffidence that grew more pronounced with time. It's strangely at odds with the bravura physical presence; in 1911, for instance, she accepted an invitation to tea with Nina Hamnett and arrived hatless, wearing one red and one blue shoe. Today this hardly seems outrageous or forward; at the time it was sufficiently daring that her shocked hostess took note. A short time later, a photo was taken of Carrington naked and posing as a living statue at Garsington Manor, standing athwart an actual stone statue in the garden. In person, she was venturesome and unconventional — even, some would argue, reckless. And the letters and diary entries are at least intermittently full of high spirits; there's very little held back.

But the artist made no such display. In 1915 she wrote Mark Gertler, "When you said that the artist's name didn't matter in a picture and you did not want to be a big artist yourself, only a creator, I felt I loved you more than I ever have before." Anonymity attracted her the way other painters seek name recognition and fame. Too, it was part of the ethos of the Omega Group — a workshop supervised by Roger Fry in which the artists (Carrington importantly among them) worked in the medieval manner, leaving their labors unsigned. On January 1, 1917, she wrote Lytton Strachey about this issue of ownership; she had been working on his portrait for two months:

I wonder what you will think of it when you see it. I sit here, almost every night, it sometimes seems, looking at your picture, now tonight it looks wonderfully good, and I am happy. But then I dread showing it. I should like to go on always painting you every week, wasting the afternoon loitering, and never, never showing you what I paint. It's marvelous having it all to oneself. No agony of the soul. Is it vanity? No, because I don't care for what they say. I have only the indecency of showing them what I have loved. It's been a happy day today.

· · ·

What did this quicksilver creature look like; how did she behave? By the social code of Bedford, her conduct was "bohemian"; she had to keep her escapades (traveling unchaperoned with men to whom she was not married, falling in love with other women) secret from her parents. When Virginia Woolf saw a stain on Lytton Strachey's pants and impishly asked him, "Is it semen?" she and the other "Bloomsberries" were doing what they could to stake out new terrain. Born in the nineteenth century, these English artists were creatures of the twentieth; when Woolf remarked that "on or about December 1910, human nature changed," she was not being wholly facetious. That declaration (in the 1924 essay "Mr. Bennett and Mrs. Brown") was militant as well as tongue-in-cheek.

So Carrington was both precocious and, at least to start with, circumspect; tradition-bound, she did what she could to break rules. The others of her circle were doing so as well. John Maynard Keynes had affairs with men before marrying in middle age; Leonard and Virginia Woolf were, in their marriage, celibate;

Duncan Grant, though unmarried, was anything but. Aldous Huxley, D. H. Lawrence, Katherine Mansfield, and Bertrand Russell (while not technically members of the Bloomsbury community) followed a similar pattern: iconoclastic in behavior, thought, and art. In her biography of Carrington, Gretchen Holbrook Gerzina sums up these contradictions: "Her life was a series of unresolved, opposing tensions, and its consistency lay in her ambivalence to many of the problems she faced; she loved truth but constantly lied; she rejected her lovers but continually lured them back; she was happiest when she painted, but her painting frequently depressed her."

In 1912 her fellow student Gertler rendered her in gouache on paper. A nineteen-year-old Carrington gazes at her would-be suitor smilingly. Her lips are red, her sweater blue, her helmet of hair clipped and brown. The background too is blue, though lighter and evoking a cloud-studded sky; the arrangement of shapes owes much to the geometry of Piero della Francesca, and the smile of coquettish amusement may be a conscious echo of Leonardo's *Mona Lisa*. The flesh is firm, cheeks full, neck strong, what we see of the figure robust. There's an almost marmoreal chill, however, to this young unyielding creature: *La Belle Dame sans Merci.*

Witness after witness reports on her particular mixture of animal magnetism and restraint; she managed to be somehow both seductive and aloof. When Aldous Huxley labels her "Bracegirdle," he is referring to the nights the two of them lay out under the stars at Garsington, her "virtue" intact although under siege. Lady Ottoline Morrell calls her "a wild moorland pony with a shock of fair hair, uncertain and elusive eyes, rather awkward in her movements," and Sacheverell Sitwell describes her with some puzzlement as having "certainly an aura attaching to her, too . . . in her distinctive yet classless appearance . . ."

Michael Holroyd, in his magisterial biography of Strachey, discusses Carrington at length:

> She was not really pretty, and certainly not beautiful — her body being made for action, like a boy's. But she radiated an extraordinary aura of attractiveness . . . Although not erudite herself, she had the charming gift of making others feel clever, drawing them out and listening with rapt attention to every syllable they spoke . . . She was alive at every point, consumed by the most vivid feelings about people, places, even things. One way or another she cared about everything, and the strength and variety of her feelings confused and wore her out.
>
> Always an elusive subject for the camera, no photograph catches the sparkling colour, the impetuosity and dynamism of her physical personality, or conveys much idea of the impression she created on others. At first sight there seemed something childish about her — rather chubby round cheeks, and clear eyes, so false-innocent, but full of light. To strangers or casual acquaintances she was most easily recognizable by her thick, light-brown hair, tinged with gold, and worn short and perfectly straight, like a Florentine page-boy's. But perhaps her most striking features were her smooth milk-white skin, her hands which had a peculiar independent character of their own, and a pair of large, intensely blue eyes, rather sunk in their sockets, and carrying an unforgettably tragic look which would light up with quick mischievous amusement.

. . .

Her first important attachment was to the painter Mark Gertler. Their letters are a complicated back-and-forth: she loves him, does not love him, adores him forever, cannot bear his touch, will not be intimate with him, and will not let him go. Soon enough she leaves him for the much older and less handsome and avowedly homosexual Lytton Strachey. Later, she marries Ralph Partridge. This was a lifelong wrangle for Gertler, and his passion for her and jealousy of others was extreme. When they met at Slade, it was, for him, a *coup de foudre*. For years thereafter they tormented each other, fighting over sex and integrity and the nature of commitment to each other and to art. A poem he wrote but did not send, in August 1916, has this opening stanza:

> If my love were not impassioned,
> or could with will be moderate,
> I could bask, in pleasant friendships'
> lukewarm sun, contentedly:
> But Love's beauty once perceived,
> mere friendship can no longer satiate:
> So when I saw your love's immensity,
> iron-coffined by virginity,
> Pain turned my love into hate.

His language has the ring of barely controlled hysteria, and from the moment he met Carrington, Gertler was enthralled. Here's a small sampling of their epistolary affair:

*Carrington to Mark* (circa December 1916): Will you not ask me to live with you often when I come back. I don't like it very much. I like it better when we are just friends. I think it makes me rather upset. But sometimes, since you care for it, I do not mind . . .

*Carrington to Mark* (London, January 5, 1917): I could hardly sleep last night through wretchedness because I am so miserable at making you unhappy. And how to explain it? . . . I want frightfully to get on with you but I feel so wretched when I am with you now . . . Dear, please for heaven's sake forgive me this wrong I am doing you.

*Mark to Carrington* (London, March 1917): You *must not* resist me physically . . . By entering into it with more lightness, even humour, you will do away with half the trouble at once and I will only appreciate your kindness and sacrifice, and love you with a beautiful love; also I will not abuse your kindness for I *quite* understand your difficulty. In doing this you will *not* be dishonest but *kind*. I will not be mislead: I never was, in fact . . . Oh, my beautiful girl!

*Mark to Carrington* (Draft of projected letter): Please do not write to me. I really mean to have done with you—You spoil my life—always have, and always shall as long as I shall know you. So I don't want to know. You think by holding my hand or giving me an occasional kiss you have a relationship with me. But there is no relationship . . .

*Carrington to Mark* (Cornwall, October 1917): May I come and see your paintings when I come back? Please, Mark. Do not think of me vilely and try and forgive me.

*Mark to Carrington* (London, October 4, 1917): It has been difficult for me to write because honestly, I do not feel the prospect of returning to you as at all enticing . . . You have treated me abominably, Carrington—always until the last moment, and it is hard not to hate you for it. Your attitude to me has been most unhuman and brutal; your selfishness appalls me — it is terrifying. And you will be just the same in the future — you can't help it. You are made like that, and I don't like you for it. By your treatments of me you have done me ever so much harm. You have sown seeds of bitterness inside me, by your brutality. I have to spend all my time now undoing what you have done to me . . . However in spite of all this I will try not to hate you and to forgive you. I will even see you sometimes if you wish it. Yes you can come and see my work whenever you like.

This sort of back-and-forth is characteristic; routinely they broke off relations, then resumed. For twelve years they blessed or berated each other and, since both of them were gifted letter writers, the correspondence makes for a compelling, if overheated, read. His letters alternate between outrage and adoration, hers between admiration and impatience. Questions of class and status enter in as well; he describes her as a Lady while he himself is just a poor Jew from the East End ghetto. Nor is Carrington always forthright. As David Garnett was to observe: "Like a child, she found it hateful to choose; and after breaking off a relationship for ever she would immediately set about starting it again."

Mark Gertler was an egotist: too self-involved and driven to be helpful as a critic of her work. Yet one of the casualties of their affair was the chance to talk about visual art; after her breach with Gertler, the company she kept was bookish, and her principal companions literary. Duncan Grant and Vanessa Bell could urge each other on with reference to their shared enterprise but, as Garnett pointed out, "It did not occur to Lytton Strachey, or to Ralph Partridge, that her painting should be put first." As the years went on, and although Carrington seemed always surrounded by men and women devoted to art, she was less and less a painter and more and more alone.

There are many issues here and much to factor in. First, and as suggested above, the cultural climate did not encourage female artists to take themselves too seriously — or, rather, to take one's art seriously was to be overearnest and not a proper wife or mother. Carrington was neither a proper wife nor mother, but there's a suspicion nevertheless that she thought herself better suited to the role of handmaiden than that of master maker; it's hard to be certain how certain she was of her gift. Augustus John and Roger Fry might praise her, but the praise was measured; the overweening egos of so many in her circle left little room for her own.

Virginia Woolf had talent of a different magnitude, perhaps, but for much of her life she too was tormented by doubt — confused as to her role in society, her sexual identity, the value of her work. For Carrington, the "Sapphic" impulse — to use the term then current — grew increasingly compelling, and she never quite decided on the kind of bodily comfort she sought or who should share her bed. Although the world of Bloomsbury was one that welcomed women, her place in it came mostly as a result of alliance with Strachey; she made small effort to be recognized for her art alone. This is paradoxical, since painting was what empowered her, and in the early years she did seem destined for success.

Again, it's worth remembering the position of women generally at the close of the Victorian era. As Woolf would write so trenchantly when imagining Shakespeare's lost sister, the chance to make a life (not to mention a living) as a female artist was a chance that few could take. More likely there'd be drudgery, small formal education or opportunity for self-expression, the dangers of childbearing and bodily assault. In our twenty-first century, things have changed, and Carrington stands in the vanguard of such alteration; part of the trail she blazed and the debt we owe her has to do with personal behavior at least as much as art.

At first, her commitment appeared unequivocal. Dismissively, in 1920, she wrote to Gerald Brenan, "If when I am 38, I am not yet an artist & think it is no good my persevering with my painting, I might have a child." Then, in 1922, she told the doting Brenan, "If I become a very good painter no one can take that from me and today I feel rather proud, rather moved from everyone, even cynical about myself, except that I wish to paint very well." Two years later she would write him (on July 25, 1924), "The solution to all my difficulties lies up stairs in my studio," and (on October 19), "I mind none of the vexations of life when I am painting." By 1932, however, she would inform her ex-lover: "I often hope I shall die at forty. I could not bear the ignominy of becoming a stout boring elderly lady with a habit of sketching in watercolours." There's a large distance traveled here, and a change—a loss—of heart.

How and why she tamped down aspiration isn't easy to assess. In retrospect it's clear that hers was an impressive gift, and what distinguishes her from, say, Stanley Spencer or Mark Gertler is that neither of those graduates from the Slade School allowed themselves a moment of masculine uncertainty as to the importance of their creative task. They took for granted—in a way that Carrington seemed unable to—the relevance of their own striving, and the egotistic syllogism: *Art matters. I matter. Therefore my art matters.* Over time she grew discouraged and tempted to give painting up.

This ice is thin to tread. She was extremely gifted in the art of portraiture, for instance, and one of the indispensable gifts of the portrait painter is to be self-effacing. We know a Rembrandt is a Rembrandt and a Frans Hals a Frans Hals; it's not as if their pictorial strategies or personalities disappear. But the face of the subject is crucial, the distinguishing traits of the sitter matter more than those of the painter (unless we're dealing with self-portraiture), and Carrington was very good indeed at disappearing from a canvas. To take just three examples—Lytton Strachey, E. M. Forster, and Gerald Brenan—the men she memorialized are distinct, each from each, and the paintings acknowledge those differences. These are (I think it fair to use the word) masterpieces of psychological acuity, and they demonstrate an intimate knowledge of the personalities on view. Strachey lies back, long fingers curled, staring left to right across the composition; Forster gazes right to left, and Brenan straight ahead. The bookish Strachey, tentative and downward-facing Forster, and sturdy Brenan wearing peasant dress could not be less alike.

On close examination, the thickness of pigment, the color-field and brushstrokes belong to one and the same artist; it's clear that Carrington stood at the easel for all three. But what we see in this trio of paintings is their subject, not their artist, and the lack of ego here is an important aspect of the works' success. This holds true as well for early portraits of her father and her brother and of later full-length portraits of Lady Strachey and the heads of Catharine Alexander, Lytton's niece Julia Strachey, Olive Penrose, and others. She had a genuine talent for the representation of character in paint.

In this regard it's interesting that she sat so rarely for herself. The pencil sketch of her own shadowed, unshorn head at seventeen and one woodcut (dated April 2, 1917) satisfied her sufficiently to keep. It may well be she painted her own face and body often, then overpainted the image or destroyed it out of pique. Yet very few major portrait painters used themselves as subjects so seldom, and it's no accident that in later years she vanished from the scene. All this suggests, again, that Carrington was self-effacing, not self-promoting, and committed to the anonymity espoused by the Omega Workshops. Routinely when she drew herself, it was as a stick figure or caricature; she did not sign her art. Some examples of it were even misattributed to the work of children or folk artists, for she could be self-consciously naïve. In any case the scrupulous analysis that she conferred on others was at best grudgingly trained on the mirror. She less and less liked what she saw.

This may be inescapable in the art of youth. Our aging selves are seldom as attractive as our young ones, and second acts seldom improve on the first. That Rembrandt painted his own crumbling flesh is part of his great and original genius; mostly what we study on museum walls is the self-portrait of an artist while still young. The youthful Albrecht Dürer and Edgar Degas proclaimed themselves as painters by studying their own unlined faces; it was a kind of calling card and an announcement of prowess. *Look at me looking,* the face seems to say. *I'll show you how much I can see.*

Although Carrington would not grow old, she would and did grow weary; a kind of lassitude that may have been engendered by depression entered in. In later years she expended most of her energy on the gardens and rooms of Ham Spray, the home she shared with Strachey. Wall by wall she festooned it with paintings and objects, its decoration reminiscent of, though more sophisticated than, Charleston—the residence of Clive and Vanessa Bell. She threw herself into the pleasurable labors of a designed domesticity, and visitors described the house as a true work of art. She made ceramic tiles for the kitchens of friends or paintings on glass as house gifts; she never lost her habit of rendering the things she saw—pencil or pen or brush always to hand. But sponged walls and stencils and cherished antiques and Staffordshire figures and bookshelves abounding do not constitute a large artistic legacy, and one cannot escape the suspicion that this particular visual artist displaced her own early ambition and allowed it, finally, to fade.

Her major and lifelong involvement was with Lytton Strachey. The writer of *Eminent Victorians*—Cambridge-educated, highly intellectual, overtly homosexual—and the girl from Bedford are the very definition of "odd couple." In 1915 they met at the Woolfs' house, Asheham, during a weekend party that included Duncan Grant. Strachey was a frequent visitor, and Carrington and another painter from Slade, Barbara Hiles—soon to be Barbara Hiles Bagenal—had been invited as well. Famously, when Strachey and Carrington went for a walk in the woods, the much older houseguest (he was thirty-five, she twenty-two) turned to kiss her. Perhaps he was attracted to the young woman's pageboy haircut and boyish figure; perhaps he was attempting—as he did a few times, haltingly — to present himself as heterosexual; perhaps he was merely being, in an offhand way, polite. But Carrington was outraged by her tall, thin, bearded companion, complaining to her friend from Slade that he was "horrid," and she seems to have determined, by way of revenge, to cut off Strachey's beard. At dawn the next day she stole into the room where he lay sleeping, scissors in hand. It's a dream of castration, a practical joke, but he woke up and stared at her and something in his steady gaze inflamed her own desire and she fell in love.

The whole makes a strange story. Think of Romeo and Juliet, of Dante and Beatrice, Petrarch and Laura, Tristan and Isolde — a magic philter, a soul-shattering glance, the Prince and Cinderella, or the Princess and the Frog. It partakes of fable and a kind of autohypnosis; it feels implausible. Yet for the rest of her life she stayed under his spell, and it was to prove an all-consuming passion. To his friends, the other charter members of the Bloomsbury community, the writer was initially dismissive of the painter, a bit chary in admitting how much she came to matter. But that weekend changed them both. Virginia Woolf would unkindly remark that, at a certain point in the evening, the two of them would go upstairs, "ostensibly to copulate," but in fact to read a chapter of Macaulay. She and Maynard Keynes and others of the circle couldn't quite believe, at first, that this mismatched-seeming couple would make each other happy or fit together hand-in-glove. But it was so. Strachey came to rely on Carrington with a reciprocated neediness, and they would be companions more or less uninterruptedly thereafter. They lived together, sharing a house, first at Tidmarsh Mill and then at Ham Spray, until his death in 1932. Theirs is one of the great love affairs of the twentieth century—a platonic pairing—and from the moment she crept into his room, scissors in hand, her romantic fate was sealed.

In her diary, Carrington records a later conversation between them (April 13, 1917):

C: I thought I had better tell Mark [Gertler], as it was so difficult going on.

L: Tell him what?

C: That it couldn't go on. So I just wrote and said it.

L. What did you say in your letter?

C: I thought you knew.

L: What do you mean?

C: I said that I was in love with you. I hope you don't mind very much.

L: But aren't you being rather romantic and are you certain?

C: There's nothing wrong about it.

L: What did Mark say?

C: He was terribly upset.

L: Did he seem angry with me?

C: No. He didn't mention you.

L: But it's too incongruous. I'm so old and diseased. I wish I was more able.

C: That doesn't matter.

L: What do you mean. What do you think we had better do about the physical.

C: Oh I don't mind about that.

L: That's rather bad. You should, I thought you did care. What about those boys, when you were young.

C: Oh that was just being young. Nothing.

L: But do you mind me being rather physically attracted.

C: I don't think you are really.

L: Why? Because of your sex.

C: Yes partly. I don't blame you. I knew it long ago and went into it deliberately.

L: They will think I am to blame.

C: They needn't know.

L: Mark will tell them.

C: No he won't.

L: But my dear aren't you being rather romantic. You see I'm so very ancient, and well—

C: It's all right. It was my fault. I knew what I was doing.

L: I wish I was rich and then I could keep you as my mistress.

C: (I was angry then inside) It would not make any difference.

L: No it wouldn't, true . . .

Leon Edel, in *Bloomsbury: A House of Lions,* summarizes their interaction thus:

> Carrington pursued Lytton, but he was willing to be pursued . . . She organized a household around him. She surrounded him with friends; she was an accomplished siren and attractive to certain kinds of men who in turn were attractive to Lytton. She brought Lytton his daily glasses of milk; she tucked him into his shawls and comforters, provided hot-water bottles, and learned to cook for him. She asked him to educate her.

• • •

That education was thorough. He had a vast library and liked to read aloud to Carrington, translating from the French. He introduced her to or enlarged upon her knowledge of the classics, Greek and Roman. To begin with, they were impoverished, but with the kind of poverty that entails trips to the country or abroad in order to economize on the expenditures of city life. Once Strachey grew solvent, moreover, he denied himself nothing—even offering his companion an annuity of one hundred pounds (a considerable sum back then) so that she could focus on the making of "pure" art. The success of *Eminent Victorians* kept the writer in funds, and rural surroundings suited them both. In her diary, on February 14, 1919, she described her days with Lytton: "All his adventures and experiences are mental and only enjoyed by himself. Outwardly, it's like the life of one of the hens. Meals dividing up the day, books read in morning, siesta, walk to Pangbourne, more books. A French lesson with me, perhaps dinner. Reading aloud. Bed and hot water bottles, and every day the same apparently. But inside, what a variety, and what fantastic doings."

The young painter traveled abroad. She did so in the time-honored fashion, in order to "expand horizons" and study her great predecessors. From Madrid, on April 15, 1919, Carrington wrote to Lytton: "This morning I spent in the Prado. How can one say what one feels when all the air has been pressed out of one's lungs through the sheer exhaustion of marveling. The portraits of Goya perhaps delighted me as much as anything."

This is the reaction of a dedicated artist, one transfixed by what she saw. Carrington was drawn as well to the folk art of Europe and America (unlike those of her contemporaries who responded more to the artifacts of Africa and Asia). But although she would admire and attempt to emulate a long line of continental masters, it's clear her eye and palette and creative sensibility were *English*—

quintessentially so. I run the risk of stereotype, but there's something fresh-faced and garden-loving about the art of Carrington; her portraits of farm workers, studies of maids, arrangements of flowers all attest to the English attitude in a way that's separable from the Spanish, Italian, or French. Her work on her houses with Strachey (first Tidmarsh Mill and then Ham Spray) and, later, on the homes of friends displays a kind of craftsmanship that's very much in the traditional Anglo-Saxon mode. William Morris and the Pre-Raphaelites belong to the same bloodline and share the same persuasion. Why should one not, they seem to say, bring color and design to walls; why not lavish attention on curtains and chairs in order to brighten dark interiors? A bookshelf with stencils or a book with decorated covers makes one happier in winter than a bookshelf or book without. When traveling, she did paint sun-drenched villages and fishing boats along the Mediterranean, but Carrington's studies of mill ponds and snow-covered fields are much more authoritative; the light is a northerly light.

One must not romanticize her life with Strachey, however; their relationship was fraught. His sexual predilections did not change, and hers remained uncertain. A twenty-three-year-old veteran of the First World War, Rex Partridge, returned from the hell of Verdun and was introduced to Strachey by a mutual friend. Of their first meeting, Partridge wrote that he had met "a painting Damsel and a great Bolshevik who would like me to strike a blow for the Cause." Most of the Bloomsbury circle had been conscientious objectors, and Partridge — rechristened "Ralph" by Lytton — could not have been mistaken for a member of that club; his animal exuberance contrasted to that of the indolent Strachey, and his good looks enchanted the writer, who wanted to keep him around. When Leon Edel remarks that Carrington "was an accomplished siren and attractive to certain kinds of men who in turn were attractive to Lytton," he refers in part to Partridge (as earlier to Gertler). She was Strachey's bait and lure while he tried to reel Partridge in.

It worked. They made a ménage à trois, with Ralph spending weekends at Tidmarsh, digging the potato fields and having his portrait painted. "Carrington loved Lytton more than ever; Lytton was falling in love with Ralph; Ralph was in love with Carrington and each one loved the other. Ralph wanted marriage." Strachey found all this convenient and urged the couple on. In an emotionally charged letter just before her wedding, Carrington wrote Strachey of the "savage, cynical fate which had made it impossible for my love ever to be used by you . . . I never could have my Moon."

Against her better judgment she did marry Partridge, and though they were in some ways a less mismatched-seeming couple than Carrington and Strachey, this arrangement too was fraught. They married on May 21, 1921, and honeymooned in Venice; by the second week Lytton joined them, and they all toured Italy. Almost from the outset, Ralph took other lovers, and by way of reciprocity the painter too looked elsewhere—growing more and more involved with her husband's best friend, Gerald Brenan. He also had fought in the First World War, in the same company as Partridge; he first had learned of Carrington in 1915, and apparently carried her image as a romantic talisman in the horrors of the trenches. When wounded and recuperating in London in 1917, he frequented the haunts of artists in the hope of meeting her.

Two years later—just after Carrington and Partridge became lovers on a walking tour of Spain—she and Brenan met.

At first their exchange of intimacies was epistolary, but by December 1919, she was writing, "I believe if one wasn't reserved, and hadn't a sense of 'what is possible' one could be very fond of certainly two or three people at a time." The triangle—moon, sun, and earth—is a geometrical figure, and its lines and angles (although the sum stays constant) can adjust. Yet there's a predictability to the orbits of the moon and earth, even if, as Carrington wrote Strachey, "I never could have my Moon." She and her husband and Strachey did manage to cohabit. While it was clear that Partridge would not gratify Lytton's sexual advances, his managerial competence soon proved indispensable to the workings of the household. He remained a faithful presence, though infidelities were frequent, and he fell in love with a black-haired beauty named Frances Marshall whom he would marry after Carrington's death and who, as Frances Partridge (1900–2004), was among the last of the "Bloomsberries" to expire. Partridge himself joined the Woolfs' Hogarth Press as of 1920. Carrington endorsed his life in London and the new romantic alliance; his subsequent marriage to Frances seems to have been successful, and he died of a heart attack in 1960. A summary of these entanglements should give some sense of their complexity and of the painter's shifting allegiance. When a third male joined the equation, however, Carrington's three-sided shape became rectangular; the complications and intersecting coordinates and stresses of alignment would grow fierce.

Gerald Brenan was a writer and a solitary, her husband's closest friend, who took two thousand books with him to a remote mountain village in Andalucía; there he could live cheaply on his wartime bonus of 250 pounds, nurse his love for Carrington, and assure her—incorrectly—that he would not be possessive. They wrote letter after letter, enflaming each other with prose. Before the two of them had consummated their affair, Ralph and therefore Lytton grew alarmed and, when Brenan returned to England and she went off to visit, intervened. The whole is a French farce of sorts, with doors being slammed and oaths being sworn and eternal fealty instant by instant proclaimed. "Gerald had reserved his *'summa inspiratio'* for Carrington and it would seem, spiritually, losing Gerald was a greater privation to Carrington than the loss of Ralph would have been, but less than the sum of the loss of Lytton and Ralph (on whom Lytton had come to depend) and the life all three had made together at Tidmarsh."

She and Brenan did become lovers, and there's a photograph of the three men—Strachey, Partridge, Brenan—sharing a blanket on a picnic. For a while, and while she painted him, things went on as before. But it was never easy; Brenan, like Gertler previously, hoped their love would be exclusive and, failing that, removed himself from the collective embrace. He kept the green dress that she wore at Watendlath (the village where she'd stayed with him) and a lock of her hair until he died; he dreamed of her, he would report, all through the 1950s. As late as 1979 he wrote to V. S. Pritchett, "I was as proud of my affair with her as I was of having been in the line at Passchendale. The tears I shed for her were, I thought, my true medals . . ."

Nor did Carrington relinquish him without regret. One has the sense that this affair cost her much more than the others, but in the end she opted for the status quo ante with Lytton and Ralph. A letter she wrote to Strachey puts her position succinctly and explains the choice she made:

> I cannot but help being lonely without seeing you, and I feel so often perhaps you miss me ... That's what Ralph doesn't feel The importance above everything [that] a work of art, and a creator of such works has for me. And yet, do you know, this morning I felt these conflicting emotions are destroying my purpose for painting. That perhaps that feeling which I have had ever since I came to London years ago now, that I am not strong enough to live in this world of people, and paint, is a feeling which has complete truth in it. And yet when I envision leaving you and going like Gerald into isolation, I feel I should be so wretched that I should never have the spirit to work.

• • •

These conflicting imperatives stayed with her: the claims of love and art. In an ideal world, perhaps, they need not have been in conflict, but Carrington appeared to feel that her life together with Strachey was an indispensable component of "my purpose for painting." Without him, she would be defenseless; with him, she felt (paradoxical though this appears) self-sufficient. In her youth and young maturity she claimed to loathe all bodily contact, and not until her mother died could she admit to satisfactions of the flesh. It takes only a passing acquaintance with Freud to notice that the two men she loved unequivocally—her semi-paralyzed father and the homosexual Strachey—were no sort of threat to her physical self; by leaving her body inviolate, they enabled the girl, then woman, to locate ardor elsewhere. Too, her protestations early on as to the value of virginity have something to do with a desire to lie prostrate instead on the altar of art. When Carrington was young, she had a kind of single-mindedness; as the years went on she grew, in terms of focus, confused.

Once she left the Slade behind, she exhibited her work infrequently, and she could be easily wounded. In 1920, when she included three of her paintings with the London Group and was reviewed, she wrote, "There is arrant bilge written in this week's Nation and Athenaeum . . . What a pass things have come to! No one can just enjoy with their eyes simply, they must argue and reason and criticize."

Again we watch the pendulum swing between independence and dependence, settling on interdependence. After the contretemps with Brenan, there would be a series of lovers (by one of whom she was made pregnant and whose child she aborted); there would be a series of women where pregnancy was not at issue and physical pleasure became at last keen. The "Sapphic" side of Carrington emerged. But the main effect, it seems, of her affair with Gerald and her increasing distance from her husband, Ralph, was to solidify the linkage with Lytton and make of that linkage a bond.

Perhaps the least conflicted of Carrington's affairs was with the daughter of the American ambassador to the Court of St. James's, an heiress from Kentucky named Henrietta Bingham. Ms. Bingham was a heartbreaker, making and missing appointments with the insouciance of the much-sought-after, and by both the genders. For the first time in her life, the painter found herself pursuing a lover rather than being pursued. Henrietta liked to sing Negro spirituals she had learned in her "old Kentucky home," accompanying herself on the mandolin and drinking copiously.

It was not an affair with a future; Strachey disapproved. But in her characteristic manner Carrington annotated for Gerald Brenan the chapter and verse of her passion, describing with great specificity the nature of her hopes, her fears and satisfactions. When finally the two women made love, she was ecstatic, writing to Alix Strachey (the wife of Lytton's brother James): "I am very much more taken with Henrietta than I have been with anyone for a long time. I feel now regret at being such a blasted fool in the past, to stifle so many lusts I had in my youth, for various females."

A pen-and-ink line drawing of a naked Henrietta, done in 1923, is an erotic proclamation; the figure stands, one hand on hip, one arm cocked and upraised in a come-hither gesture, and wearing only heels. In a letter to Julia Strachey, Carrington described the way that shoes could make her feel: "Under the excuse of examining the buckles, I gave them a delicate stroke, and the thrill that ran down my spine, my dear! I can hardly describe." There's a drawing of a naked Julia Strachey also, lying down and wearing pearls. She seems a kind of odalisque, half Goya's *Naked Maja* and half Manet's *Olympia,* with both halves wholly ready for the pleasures of the flesh. Carrington began her career as artist with prize-winning studies at the Slade of female nudes; these drawings offer an elaboration of that theme, but with carnal knowledge added in.

Here it's worth remembering how young the painter was when she came to her teachers' attention and how relatively youthful still in the early 1920s when proclaiming her discovery of sex. All her life she hated menstruation; she seems to have been beaten by her governess when a child; the men who early on attempted to seduce her were self-regarding, no matter how rapt. Her love affairs with male partners—including the last, with Beakes Penrose (which resulted in the pregnancy from which she recoiled and which, with the help of Strachey and Partridge, she terminated rapidly)—afforded her some gratification. But it's fair to say, as she herself said, that the relations with "the other half" were tortuous, burdened by the inadequacies of response and failed high expectations. With Henrietta, however, what she saw was what she got.

As time went by, and as she matured, these yearnings grew less keen. Beakes Penrose with his sailboat and Gerald Brenan (whom Carrington called "Shelley") did retain a hold on her, as did the women with whom she made love and the man with whom she celibately lived. As she confided to her diary:

> Happiness in life is largely a matter of time relationships— some experiences come too early others too late with relation to ones [sic] other situations and affairs or to one's age. At 37 one should be settling down over tea cups, bottling gooseberries, instead of which I have Shelley cravings to sail and leave these quiet rural scenes for Greek Islands. Ridiculous.

The photograph of Carrington balancing naked athwart a statue in the gardens of Garsington Manor was adapted by Vanessa Bell some twelve years afterward for a panel titled *Bacchanale*. Bell's figure was hermaphroditic, reflecting what she recognized in Strachey's friend, even if the girl had not yet seen herself as such. As Virginia Woolf's *Orlando* suggests, there was a good deal of cross-dressing and bisexual role-playing in the world of Bloomsbury. Although the painter ran the household, "a sort of overboiling seizes me sometimes when I am interrupted in my studio to turn off the water, & have to put logs on the fires & order all the meals, to hear these perpetual shrieks in the sitting room & nobody stirring—what they call—a finger—to do any work in the house."

"Please do not understand me too quickly," as André Gide remarked. A delayed or deferred comprehension may well prove truer in the end than understanding that comes quick. Carrington was always a bit of a cipher, and she took time to decode. What matters, I think, is that she came to terms not so much with ambivalence as with a twinned allegiance, and that toward the close of her life she seems to have accepted without rancor the doubled state of things.

What, then, are we to make of this remarkable figure, this apostle of one of the "Cambridge Apostles" who walked the tightrope teeteringly between a public and private career? If only as a letter writer and keeper of journals Carrington proved notable: vivaciously alert to the world around her and the world within. But many professional record keepers—David Garnett, Harold Nicolson and Vita Sackville-West, the Woolfs and Bells among them—were more central to the community of Bloomsbury. And there are many amateurs—Frances Partridge, for example, or Angelica Garnett—whose records of the place and time reward our close attention. Memoirs and studies of that period are hydra-headed still; everyone, it seems, has something to remember or something to observe about the habits and behavior of the "House of Lions." The children and grandchildren of those who lived in Gordon Square or cavorted at Asheham and Sissinghurst add yearly to our knowledge of their personalities. The anecdotes accrete. What remains in the case of Carrington is not so much the gossip as the work she left behind: the drawings and paintings themselves.

There's limitless potential, and a kinetic achievement. She had both talent and technical skill; her best work is as good as any then being produced. She was easily the equal of, and a better draftsman than, more celebrated contemporaries such as Duncan Grant and the queen of Bloomsbury, Vanessa Bell. The range of her preserved endeavors—from crowded market scenes to intricate ink drawings of single figures, from woodcuts and stencils to paintings on glass, from frescoes to shop signs and fireplace tiles, from landscapes to portraits and still lifes of flowers—is impressively wide. As a portrait painter Carrington lays legitimate claim to be an heir of English portraitists such as Gainsborough and Reynolds; as a landscape painter she descends from Constable and Turner. I don't mean by this that the line of descent is direct, or that those earlier English artists were as important to this painter as their continental counterparts. Yet she's in the tradition of the artist and the artisan within the "green and pleasant land" of Blake's "Jerusalem," and British to the core. At her finest, Carrington produced vivid interpretations of the people and landscapes dear to her; even her casual efforts look sure-fingered and inventive. As the director of the Tate, John Rothenstein, asserts, she's "the most neglected serious painter of her time."

An early landscape painting—the Mill at Tidmarsh—makes the case. Painted in 1918, it measures twenty-eight inches by forty inches and is oil on canvas; it hangs in a private collection. The house that she and Strachey shared is offered up as a locus of

joy, though perhaps the black swans in the foreground are fore-
boding, even ominous; the mill with its bright orange roofs and
chimneys and small-paned windows is reflected—refracted—in
the pond. An upright shingled structure on the right side of the
canvas points darkly down in the water as well; the bottom of
the composition mirrors the top half. A sluiceway off the River
Pang bisects the property; in the center of the canvas there's an
egg-shaped oval (half aperture, half reflection) where the stream
courses under the mill.

It is as though the house wears a face—the black tunnel serving as mouth, the rooftop windows eyes. There are gardens and
flowering trees at both sides of the canvas; reeds sprout from the
stream, and the blue sky is dotted with clouds (or the gray sky
is shot through with blue). A dead tree rises leaflessly behind the
orange roof, its branches fanning off the upper canvas edge. The
palette resembles the one deployed in the portrait of Strachey
from 1916; the two paintings feel, although not coeval, related.
Both renderings are assured; together they display full knowledge
of the landscape, house, and man. The absolute control of line,
composition, and color propose a kind of mastery; this is creative
interpretation of the very highest order, and Carrington makes of
"the art of youth" an admirable first act.

So it's doubly strange she accomplished so little and is so little
known. The image of the Mill at Tidmarsh seems emblematic of
its artist: half sturdily constructed and half a wavering reflection
of what was built by others. There's visual decisiveness yet an uncertainty here. Half of the structure is solid; the mirroring half
looks adrift. If Stephen Crane seemed conscious and dismissive
of dichotomy, prepared to use his pen turn by turn in the service

of commerce or art, this woman was ambivalent—never quite insisting on the professional importance of what she made and never quite consigning her own work to irrelevance. Tentative yet fierce, self-negating yet declarative, Carrington leaves us wondering what might have been had she known a second act. What's clear is the talent; what's unclear is the use she made of it and how untrammeled her gift. At the very least she left us with a garland of wonderful paintings; she wears that garland now.

Lytton Strachey had always been sickly. His digestive tract was delicate, his constitution weak. He was, no doubt, hypochondriacal as well. But those who tended to his dietary needs or fended off his daily complaints had come to take for granted that the writer and his catalogue of troubles would continue. What killed him in the end was stomach cancer: undiagnosed. As we have seen, he was calling himself "old and diseased" to Carrington as early as 1917; when he was an actual invalid, he bore his sufferings bravely. In 1931, at fifty-one, he began to discuss the disposal of things, telling her, "Remember, all the bird books and flower books are yours . . . after I am dead, it would be important." He had less than a year left to live.

On Thursday, January 21, 1932, when she knew that Strachey was going to die, Carrington tried to kill herself. She sat in her car and turned on the engine and hoped for asphyxiation. Her diary reports on this in detail, and it is wrenchingly sad:

> I saw from his [Lytton's] face he had no hope. He slept without any discomfort or pain. A hatred for nurse Phillips came on me. I cannot remember now anything except watching Lytton's

pale face and his close shut eyes lying on the pillows and Pippa
standing by his bed. Sleeping with his mouth open. Ray arrived.
Cars came backwards and forwards on the gravel. 'There must
be nightwatches. Pippa will stay with him till 12 o'clock. Then
I till 3 o'clock. Ralph till 6 o'clock and then you after 6 o'clock.'
At 3 o'clock I saw James outside on the landing. I had not slept.
I went in and asked nurse Mooney if there was any chance of
his living, she said: 'Oh no, I don't think so now.' I gave him a
kiss on his cold forehead, it was damp and cold. I gave Ralph a
kiss and asked him not to come and wake me. I saw him sit by
the fire, and sip some tea in Lytton's room. James went downstairs. I walked very quietly down the passage and down the
back stairs. It was half past three. The house was quiet and outside the moon shone in the yard, through the elms across the
barns. The garage door was stuck open I could hardly move it.
Every movement seemed to screech through the still night air.
At last I got the doors closed . . . I got in the car. I started it up
one minute after the milking machine which was half past five
by the car clock, but that is ten minutes fast. I was terrified by
the noise. Once it nearly stopped so I had to turn on the pet-
rol more. There seemed no smell. I got over in the back of the
car and lay down and listened to the sound of the crying below
me, and the noise of the milking machine puffing way outside.
At last I smelt it was beginning to get rather thick. I turned on
the light in the side of the car and looked at the clock. Only ten
minutes had gone. However Ralph would probably not come
exactly at 6 o'clock. The windows of the car looked foggy and a
bit misty. I turned out the light again, and lay down. Gradually
I felt rather sleepy, and the buzzing noise grew fainter and further off. Rather like fainting I remember thinking. And not
what Ellie had told me about a pain in one's throat. I thought
of Lytton, and was glad to think I shouldn't know any more.
Then I remember a sort of dream which faded away.

Suddenly, long after, waking up in my bed with a buzzing in my ears, and Dr. Starkey Smith holding my arm and injecting a syringe. I cried, 'No, no, go away,' and pushed him and his hand away and saw him vanish like the Cheshire cat. Then I looked and saw my bedroom window and it was daylight, and Ralph was there. Ralph held me in his arms and kissed me and said: 'How could you do it?' I felt *angry* at being back after being in a very happy dream. Sorry to be awake again . . . I must confess I felt defrauded and angry that fate had cheated me in such a way and brought me back again. I got up at 12 o'clock and went into Lytton's room. He was still sleeping, breathing very deeply and fast. Pippa sat in a chair. I went and sat in the chair and watched him. 'So this is death,' I kept saying to myself. The two nurses moved about behind the screen . . . We stood there. I do not know for how long . . . But then he breathed again, fainter. Suddenly he breathed no more and nurse MacCabe put her hand on his heart under the clothes and felt it. I looked at his face: it was pale as ivory. I went forward and kissed his eyes, and his forehead. They were cold.

She would not be consoled. Strachey's cremated ashes were removed by James, his brother, although Carrington had hoped to plant them beneath the garden's ilex tree. She went through the motions of managing things, but her diary is comfortless and sorrowful, its cadences those of the self-doomed. This, from February 11 of that year:

We couldn't have been happier together. For every mood of his instantly made me feel in the same mood. All gone. And I never told him or showed him how utterly I loved him. And now there is nobody, darling Lytton, to make jokes with about Tiber and the horse of the ocean, no one to read me Pope in the evenings, no one to work on the terrace. No one to write letters to, oh my very darling Lytton.

Carrington wrote about and to him obsessively. The next day's entry includes these lines:

Everything I look at brings back a memory of you. Your brown writing case that I bought you in Aix. Your clothes that I chose with you at Carpentier and Packer. All our pictures and furniture that we chose together. Oh darling did you know how I adored you. I feared often to tell you because I thought you might feel encumbered by your 'incubus.' I know you didn't want to feel me dependent on you. I pretended so often I didn't mind staying alone. When I was utterly miserable as the train went out and your face vanished. You were the kindest dearest man who ever lived on this earth. No one can ever be your equal for wit and gaiety. And you transported me by your magical conversations and teaching into a world which no one could have dreamt of; it was so fantastically happy and amusing. What does anything mean to me now without you. I see my paints and think it is no use, for Lytton will never see my pictures now, and I cry.

On February 16, 1932, she wrote:

At last I am alone. At last there is nothing between us. I have been reading my letters to you in the library this evening. You are so engraved on my brain that I think of nothing else. Everything I look at is part of you. And there seems no point in life now you are gone. I used to say: 'I must eat my meals properly as Lytton wouldn't like me to behave badly when he was away.' But now there is no coming back . . .

And I thought as I threw the rubbish on the bonfire 'So that's the end of his spectacles. Those spectacles that have been his companions all these years. Burnt in a heap of leaves.' And those vests the 'bodily companions' of his days now are worn by a carter in the fields. In a few years what will be left of him? A few books on the shelves, but the intimate things that I loved, all gone.

And soon even the people who knew his pale thin hands and the texture of his thick shiny hair, and grisly beard, they will be dead and all remembrance of him will vanish. I watched the gap close over others but for Lytton one couldn't have believed (because one did not believe it was ever possible) that the world would go on the same.

It did not. The diary continues in this vein, with elegiac eloquence. After his death she wrote poems as well. Here's one called "Advice to Oneself":

> Turn down the wick!
> Your night is done
> There rises up another sun
> Another day is now begun
> Turn down your wick.
> Turn down the lamp!
> Time to expire.
> 'Body and soul' end your tune
> Retreat my pale moon,
> And turn out your lamp.

In her diary she cut and pasted the stanzas that Chidiock Tichborne composed in the Tower of London before his execution—

The first manuscript page of *The Red Badge of Courage*. The working title, "Private Fleming/His Various Battles," has been canceled, but there are few other changes in the draft.

*Stephen Crane Papers, Special Collections, University of Virginia Library*

Stephen Crane at his desk in Brede Place, the house in Sussex that became his final home.

*Stephen Crane Collection, Special Collections Research Center, Syracuse University Library*

Crane in the garb of a war correspondent on fake rocks
in a photography studio in Athens, 1897.

Cora at the same place and time (May 22, 1897), inscribed "To me old pal Stevie,
with best wishes" and signed with her professional pseudonym, "Imogene Carter."

Carrington's self-portrait, done at age seventeen in 1910, before she cropped her hair. *Courtesy of the National Portrait Gallery, London*

Her bedroom at Ham Spray, with its ornamental fireplace and portraits on the wall—among them the portrait of Lytton Strachey in an alcove by the bed.

*From a private collection*

Carrington and a seated Strachey, happily at home.

*Courtesy of the National Portrait Gallery, London*

A naked Carrington posing athwart a statue in the garden of Garsington Manor.
At the time she was the guest of Lady Ottoline Morell. *From a private collection*

Black swans on the sluiceway and the Mill at Tidmarsh, painted in 1918.

*From a private collection*

George and Ira with DuBose Heyward. On the left, "Dear Ira—As long as we're all autographing, I'd like to write, what it is hard to say—that I'm very proud of you. With love, George, 'Porgy and Bess,' Boston." On the right, "For my lyric twin, Ira, with admiration and every good wish from DuBose, Boston, Sept. 30, 1935."

*Courtesy of Ira and Leonore Gershwin Trusts*

George Gershwin in and as a self-portrait, with frame and pipe.

*Courtesy of Ira and Leonore Gershwin Trusts*

George Gershwin conducting at rehearsal with the Los Angeles Philharmonic,
February 1937. *Courtesy of Ira and Leonore Gershwin Trusts*

The little British boy who has learned to read, 1948.

*Kurt Delbanco*

The apprentice author on the beach at Martha's Vineyard, 1964.

*Courtesy of Peter Simon*

with its despairing refrain: "And now I live, and now my life is done." And she copied out a couplet from Sir Henry Wotton, in 1627, "Upon the Death of Sir Albert Morton's Wife":

He first deceased, she for a little tried
To live without him, liked it not and died.

On March 10, Carrington visited Rosamond Lehmann, seeming peaceful and oddly at ease; she must have made up her mind. The next day, wearing Lytton's purple dressing gown instead of her own yellow one, the painter killed herself. Earlier, she had borrowed a shotgun, saying she needed to shoot rabbits from the window since they were spoiling the lawn. As had been the case before, with her attempt at self-asphyxiation, this second attempted suicide was not immediately fatal. At first she failed to release the safety catch. Then, with the gun repositioned—its butt on the floor and barrel pointed at her side—she failed to hit her heart. The Ham Spray gardener heard the shot, then heard her groans and telephoned the doctor and Ralph Partridge.

By the time he and Frances, driven by David Garnett, arrived from London, Carrington was semicomatose from pain and the morphine given to control it. Eighteen days before her thirty-ninth birthday, at quarter past two on March 11, 1932, she died.

In the summer of 1980, my uncle—an art dealer in London—invited me and my family to Charleston, the country home of Vanessa and Clive Bell. It has since been restored, but then was being occupied by Vanessa's daughter, Angelica Garnett (1918–2012). My wife and I and our two young children were spending the summer in Sussex; we were glad for the excursion and grateful for the chance to see this fabled place. One of the central habitations of the Bloomsbury community, with handmade furniture and crockery, stenciled walls and painted floors and beds, it had fallen into (let's put it kindly) disrepair. Shards of shattered roof tiles lay along the walkway; vines had a choke hold on shutters; it must have been years since the last coat of paint, and the water-stained plaster had cracked.

Ms. Garnett was in her early sixties, polite and severe and surrounded by cats. She was embarking on an effort to raise money to preserve the house, and I shamelessly suggested I might help. She seemed pleased to see my uncle, who from time to time had represented her mother's artist-lover and her own actual father, Duncan Grant. Grant had also been the lover of David Garnett, her husband, and it was years before she would be told the true nature of her parentage; she reports on this in her acid-edged memoir, *Deceived with Kindness.* All the women of the Stephen clan were beautiful, all of them snobbish and troubled, and Vanessa's daughter's life was not a simple one; she died only recently, a nonagenarian, in the South of France. For much of that wet afternoon, she and my uncle talked about the Sackville-Wests, the weather, and what they both considered the "deplorable" condition of contemporary art.

I'd worked in his gallery some years before, trying to decide if I might make a career out of buying and selling paintings; it was not a graft that took. While my wife kept our daughters occupied, I wandered past the patched-together furniture and leaking mullioned windows and into the various bedrooms where the various partners had busily enacted their complex mating rituals, all of them well chronicled. I'd known, for example, that our hostess had been married to her unacknowledged father's considerably younger lover before I shook her hand. The rooms had the smell of wet cats. The curtains were torn, the couch springs sprung, and the throw rugs tattered; this was a tarnished shrine. Yet when she went to visit Charleston, under the spell of its eminent escapees from the Victorian Age, Carrington exclaimed, "Never, never have I seen quite such a wonderful place!"

It did not seem that way to me. We made small talk, drank cold tea, discussed again the prospect of a fund-raising drive for restoration of the house; I promised to do what I could in America, and Ms. Garnett said, "Thank you very much." The paintings that remained on walls were either her personal favorites or those that no one else wanted. We took our leave. Driving off, my uncle said, "What rubbish; rubbish is all she has left."

But the place is now restored. As was, at the last minute, the home the Ramsays occupy in Virginia Woolf's *To the Lighthouse* (when the cleaning ladies come and scrub in the "Time Passes" section), Charleston has been rescued from oblivion. The gardens are well tended now, the house repaired and repainted, much of the furniture and many of the books and paintings and cups and saucers retrieved. Glad ghosts dance again on the bright-colored floors, or wander past the plantings. Here's Vanessa picking flowers and arranging them in ripe profusion, Clive and Leonard playing chess. There are Maynard Keynes and Roger Fry and Morgan Forster reading in their rocking chairs, Virginia joshing Lytton Strachey as together they gossip and smoke. Most of them are slender; all of them wear hats. Here's Duncan Grant at an easel and Desmond MacCarthy at a writing desk; Harold Nicolson and

Vita Sackville-West, "Bunny" Garnett and Violet Trefusis and vanished shades too numerous to name. Here are Woolf's fictional
Ramsays with their brood of children, the poet Augustus Carmi-
chael, the atheist Charles Tansley, the painter Lily Briscoe. And
hovering above it all is the bright art and image of Carrington
herself.

A coda at chapter's close: Mark Gertler—who fell so cataclys-
mically in love with Carrington while both attended the Slade
School—had an important early career as artist; his pictures (particularly the oil portraits of family members and the Jewish community in which he was raised) were exhibited and praised. He
was a rising star of realism in his twenties and could make a living
from his art. As time went on, however, Gertler fell out of fashion
and had more and more trouble earning the money with which
to purchase canvases and paint. Though he never ceased experi-
menting and was always hard at work, he grew discouraged and
withdrawn.

There are parallel histories here. Two years after his death,
in 1939, an exhibition was held in the Leicester Galleries, then at
the Ben Uri Gallery in 1944; a large memorial show took place in
1949 at the Whitechapel Art Gallery. As would be true for Carrington—though in her case even more slowly—it was not until
the 1960s that collectors and museums began to vie for Gertler's
work. He now commands prices at auction that dwarf what he
earned while alive.

The painter was tubercular. In April 1920 in a fit of coughing
he spat blood; in November he collapsed. He spent time in a sana-
torium in Scotland and was often hospitalized and never wholly

hale again. In later years he suffered from migraines, depression, and shortage of breath. Like his sometime-admirer D. H. Lawrence, he was part of the last generation to be severely affected by tuberculosis; soon after his death, the drugs that provided a cure became widely available, and sanatoriums shut down.

The postmortem performed on Gertler, however, revealed that the old "wasting disease" had healed completely. What killed him instead was gas poisoning. Unlike the first of our artists—the consumptive Stephen Crane, dead in 1900—this painter chose the exit Carrington had taken several years before. (Virginia Woolf too would take her own life, submersing herself in the River Ouse after weighting her pockets with stones.) On the twenty-third of June 1939, Mark Gertler placed a mattress near a gas stove and a gas ring in his studio and, having locked the door, lay down. When he was found—dead for some hours—the stove and gas ring both were turned on full, unlit.

One of our subjects died of consumption; another was a suicide. Neither reached the age of forty; nor would our third and last.

# 4

## George Gershwin

"Here lies the body of George Gershwin, American Composer.
Composer? American?"

— GEORGE GERSHWIN, IN RESPONSE TO A 1925 *Vanity Fair*
REQUEST THAT HE COMPOSE HIS OWN EPITAPH

THE NATURE OF STEPHEN CRANE'S literary achievement is, as we have seen, open to discussion; the reputation of Dora Carrington is increasing but not large. We cannot say for certain if their "second acts" would have entailed a falling-off or growth. Might the writer have continued in the high mode of inventiveness, the painter continued to paint? Or—at twenty-eight and thirty-eight—had they exhausted their creative excellence and embarked upon decline?

These are reasonable questions, yet the answers must be moot. *What if* is by its very nature closed as well as open to conjecture. "What now, what more?" is Faust's great challenge to Mephisto and best left unasked. But in the case of our third artist, George Gershwin (1898–1937), such a line of inquiry is almost unavoidable; one cannot help but wonder what would have happened next. The upward thrust of his career seemed, in effect, unstoppable — or, rather, what stopped him was death. *What if, what else, what next?*

It's the problem posed by every man and woman dead in the throes of invention while still at the top of his or her form. If only in terms of the number of notes he wrote down in his final months, Franz Schubert was remarkable; no professional copyist (much less a composer creating what he on the instant transcribed) could have managed more. Wolfgang Amadeus Mozart had, it's clear, intimations of mortality — and his exuberant output near life's end derived in part from that awareness: the febrile rush of inspiration kept him bent above the pages of a score. George Gershwin too was working; he collapsed almost literally at the piano keyboard and the conductor's podium; he was full of projects in his final days. He did complain, in his last period, of headaches and exhaustion — but those who knew him thought it likely that he would recover; a trip to Europe or a week of tennis would no doubt prove restorative, and he'd be back onstage again with his customary élan. He'd been down-and-out before, but always only briefly, and the trajectory was always, only, up . . .

This held true from the beginning. Of our three representative figures, Gershwin is the one with the least promising origins and the greatest ensuing success. From the modest house at 242 Snediker Avenue in Brooklyn where he was born, to penthouse apartments in Manhattan and lavish suites in Hollywood, his is the career path of the American dream. Prosperity was new to him, and as soon as it arrived, he embraced its tailored trappings; with a starlet on his arm and an expensive cigar in his manicured hand, he became the very image of a dashing young celebrity. The play-boy romancer and man-about-town were roles Gershwin took to smilingly; his name glowed in actual lights. Photographers trailed him; gossip columnists made much of him; when he traveled, he traveled first class.

Crane and Carrington belonged to the solid middle strata of society; in America and England their childhood homes were large. The family Gershwin had no such firm grounding. His father, Morris (Moishe) Gershowitz, came by himself to the United States from St. Petersburg in 1890. His mother, Rosa Bruskin, left Russia in 1892. The two immigrants met again in New York (according to family lore, they had known each other in St. Petersburg) and were married on July 21, 1895. George Gershwin—the second of the couple's four children—was born on September 26, 1898, as Jacob Gershvin, the name Gershowitz had assumed upon arrival in America. After he became a professional musician; he would change the spelling of the family name to "Gershwin"; his older brother, Ira (whose given name was Israel), and the others followed suit.

Poverty was, early on, an issue; hard work was a necessity, not choice. Gershwin's father "was, at the time of his marriage, a foreman in a factory that made fancy uppers for women's shoes. But in the next twenty years he moved his family . . . no less than twenty-eight times as his occupations shifted—part owner of a Turkish bath on the Bowery, part owner of a restaurant on Third Avenue near 129th Street, part owner of another restaurant on the Lower East Side, owner of a cigar store, owner of a billiard parlor, of a bakery, even a venture into bookmaking at Belmont Park . . ." Though they were never destitute, the family was elevated by their children's earnings to true privilege; not for nothing are so many of the Gershwin brothers' songs about a realized dream.

That dream was of increase and plenty: achievement unalloyed. The art of youth appears incarnate in this artist who wrote "Swanee" when not yet twenty-one. It was recorded by Al Jolson some months later, on January 8, 1920. This first act sold hundreds of thousands of copies, and it proved a sturdy rung on the ladder of success. As songwriter, composer, performer, Gershwin has few, if any, equals in this nation's history, and none who came to prominence so young. When I asked William Bolcom—himself no small musical presence—to name a great American opera, he said there were six of them. And their names were *Porgy and Bess, Porgy and Bess, Porgy and Bess, Porgy and Bess, Porgy and Bess,* and, finally, *Porgy and Bess.*

From Gershowitz to Gershvin to Gershwin is a not-uncommon passage for those who made their immigrant way in the brave new world. Here too, in this third instance, there's a distinction to draw. Crane's father was a Methodist minister, and Carrington was raised in the stiffly pious Church of England fashion, but Gershwin was decisively a Jew. In the beginning he flirted with the Yiddish musical theater; in later years he took glad part in the Jewish Mafia of songwriting and theatrical luminaries (think of Harold Arlen, Irving Berlin, Howard Dietz, Yip Harburg, Lorenz Hart, George Kaufman, Jerome Kern, Oscar Levant, Richard Rodgers, Arthur Schwartz, and others). He would confront anti-Semitism both in America and Europe. He considered writing—and even, in 1929, signed a contract with the Metropolitan Opera for—a

Jewish opera, *The Dybbuk*. (This was a project abandoned, largely for copyright reasons; no extant sketches survive.) But the point to make about his early years is that, although impoverished, the Gershwin children were encouraged—*expected*—to make music. It was part of the ambient air. As quickly as they could afford one, the family acquired a piano, which older brother Ira was supposed to learn to play. As John S. Wilson reports, "When he was twelve, his mother bought a second-hand upright piano, partly because her sister had one, partly with the idea of starting Ira on lessons. As soon as the piano had been hoisted up through the window of their second-floor apartment, George was at the keyboard playing a popular tune of the day."

In a reminiscence, "My Brother," Ira recollects that moment. His last sentence is a characteristic understatement, tongue-in-cheek and wry:

> I remember being particularly impressed by his left hand. I had no idea he could play and found out that despite his roller skating activities, the kid parties he attended, and the many street games he participated in (with an occasional resultant bloody nose) he had found time to experiment on a player-piano at the home of a friend on Seventh Street . . . Although our piano was purchased with my taking lessons in mind, it was decided George might prove the brighter pupil.

To Ira words came easily. Their younger sister, Frances ("Frankie"), was a singer and a dancer and, briefly, a performer; the fourth child, Arthur, played the violin. This is the sort of cultural "surround" that typifies the Jewish immigrant family, no matter how empty its purse. "The process that transformed Izzy Baline, who arrived from Russia at the age of five and grew up in extreme poverty, into Irving Berlin would be hard to reproduce today; yet it was emblematic of a whole generation, and served Gershwin as a prototype for his own journey." His entrepreneurial father might have been a *luftmensch*, full of unrealized projects, and his mother a taskmistress, but both of them honored the arts. When their talented boy's occupation proved commercially rewarding, his parents dropped all objections they might otherwise have raised as to his line of work.

Young George seemed wedded to the piano from the start. He was the natural, the crowd-pleaser, the prodigy, and at fifty cents a session the delight of local ladies who gave him his first lessons. Soon he advanced to a teacher who could command three times that much — $1.50 a lesson — and at fourteen years old commenced to study with Charles Hambitzer, who was, said Gershwin, "the first great musical influence in my life."

That admiration was reciprocated, and it lasted till his teacher's death (also premature, in the flu epidemic, at the age of thirty-seven in 1918). As Hambitzer wrote in a letter to his sister, "The boy is a genius without a doubt; he's just crazy about music and can't wait until it's time to take his lessons. No watching the clock for this boy. He wants to go in for this modern stuff, jazz and what not. But I'm not going to let him for a while. I'll see that he gets a firm foundation in the standard music first."

The linkage of the "modern stuff, jazz and what not" with "the standard music" would come to signify the particular "genius" of this particular artist; it's as good a description as any of

Gershwin's doubled aspiration and of his achievement. Importantly, those opposing aims were with him in his formative years, and he pursued them both. At first he seems, under Hambitzer's tutelage, to have prepared for a concert career; soon he branched out into "song-plugging"—playing tunes for singers who might purchase and perform them—and then into composition for nightclubs and Broadway revues. The present point, however, is that he started early; in retrospect the street-smart urchin and the concertizing virtuoso were cut from the same bolt of cloth. The arrival of a piano empowered but did not engender his gift; it is as though that "second-hand upright" swinging through the upstairs window proved prophetic of the soaring soon to come. For the rest of his life he would sit at a keyboard—in dressing gown or evening clothes, in private or in public, and well into the night.

This kind of precocious commitment to music is almost a sine qua non of young talent. I know of no important pianist who commenced to play the instrument past the age of ten. Gershwin remembered standing barefoot and in overalls outside a penny arcade on 125th Street when he was six; an automatic piano was playing Anton Rubinstein's "Melody in F." "The peculiar jumps in the music held me rooted," he said, and the long line of youthful composer-performers (consider, among many, Ludwig von Beethoven, Frédéric Chopin, Franz Liszt, Felix Mendelssohn, Wolfgang Amadeus Mozart, Sergei Rachmaninov, and Clara Wieck Schumann) expanded to include a six-year-old American. Always he was listening; always he wanted to play. With Hambitzer's encouragement, he attended recitals and full orchestra performances, where he acquired "the habit of intensive listening." Later he claimed, "I had gone to concerts and listened not only with my ears . . . but with my nerves, my mind, my heart. I had listened so earnestly that I became saturated with the music . . . Then I went home and listened in memory. I sat at the piano and repeated the motifs."

The boy embarked on a largely self-taught course of study of harmony and composition; as a result, no doubt, there were those who later questioned his musical education. He was better playing Gershwin than the work of others, and through much of his career he was dogged by critical dismissiveness, a refusal to take seriously the work of a composer neither graduated from a conservatory nor classically trained. Gershwin's true academy was Tin Pan Alley and the clutch of writers employed by Jerome H. Remick and Company. The firm was located on West Twenty-eighth Street, between Broadway and Sixth Avenue, and he started working there as a song-plugger as early as 1914.

As he told an interviewer in 1925, "I got my first job with a musical concern when I was fifteen years old. A boy friend who was with the Remick Company told me of a vacancy for a piano player, one who could read notes readily, to play over songs to be tried out. I got the job at $15 a week and stayed there two years. All the time, however, I was working at my compositions." What he learned while playing "songs to be tried out" — ragtime piano, improvisation, the melodic configuration and rhythms of black composers such as James Reese Europe and Will Vodery — he would make masterful use of in the years to come.

Here are some recollections from those who knew him young. His first major collaborator, Irving Caesar (the lyricist for "Swanee"), writes:

George was very sweet and very soft and quite sensitive, but he had great faith and confidence in his music, and that was as it should be. There was nothing modest about him. I don't mean that he was overbearing, but he had self-confidence, and rightly so. For when George sat down at the piano, there was no one who could move you as George would. It was very difficult to put your finger on his talent because it lapsed over into the serious field, but there's no doubt that he blazed a trail for all popular musicians. His was a unique talent. He was in a class by himself. Isn't that enough?

His sister, Frances, writes:

When we'd dance, he loved to trick me into rhythms by going off beat and trying to catch me. I had been a dancer and had a very good sense of rhythm, but he was a beautiful dancer. George used to come home after rehearsals with Fred Astaire and would show me the steps he'd learned from Fred. He did it beautifully because he was so well coordinated.

Yes, my mother was unhappy when he made music his work. She thought one son should be a doctor, one son a lawyer — the usual thing, especially in Jewish families. But George was making a living, and by the time Ira was doing it, they didn't object — they understood it a little more. My mother was against it, for George, but she didn't make it so strong that he didn't do it. Yet he would have done it anyway; he had a will of his own.

And Kay Swift, perhaps Gershwin's major romantic attachment, describes the intensity of his nonmusical interests:

George was always an enthusiast, steamed up with the essentials of anything. A play would do it. A painting. Riding. He did it well. He smoked a cigar at the same time and I told him it doesn't go with riding a horse. An instructor somewhere up the Hudson had said to him while he was learning, "Tummy in, tummy out. Tummy in, tummy out." That was how you trotted. Sounds like something Gilbert and Sullivan would write.

Dancing was just natural with him. He didn't take any lessons. He was a free spirit, but very conventional where his family was concerned—although he was always blazing ahead . . . George always put all of himself into everything he was doing. He always had complete concentration.

The range of Gershwin's endeavors was wide, the scope of achievement broad. Though single-minded in his focus on a career in music, he had other interests as well. He rode and swam and golfed and boxed with omnivorous enthusiasm; he danced and played tennis with skill. The profession of composer is a sedentary one, and his athletic diversions no doubt offered physical release from long hours at the keyboard: a kind of counterpoint. He read; he liked to travel; he wrote with colloquial flair. He was a serious amateur painter and, soon enough, a collector. His eye for art (particularly the Post-Impressionists and the Fauves) was keen; he acquired work by, among others, Derain, Dufy, Kandinsky, Kokoschka, Léger, Masson, Modigliani, Pascin, Picasso, Rouault, and Vlaminck. With his thick wallet and free-ranging alertness, he also acquired African sculpture and the work of such Americans as Thomas Hart Benton and Maurice Sterne.

His own art stands up to scrutiny. *Self-Portrait in a Checkered Sweater* (1936) is much more than a Sunday painter's rendering; it bears comparison with Carrington's oil portraits, as do the studies of Arnold Schoenberg and Jerome Kern, done in the subsequent year. To call him a Renaissance man is to overstate the case, but he tried his hand at many modes of expression, and each of them intensely. As Edward G. Robinson wrote, in a memorial tribute: "Apart from his genius in music, he had a genius for living . . . I value above all things the memory I have of George. George — high-spirited, almost boyish — simple — unaffected — lovable — and charged with the power to make all things, great and small, absorbing and significant."

No matter what Gershwin engaged in, he engaged it fully. His appetites were large. As voracious in his consumption of ice cream as of romantic partners, he seemed to have no limit to his hunger or ebullience. Such hunger was not indiscriminate, however; he was careful about his diet and to the end of his brief life stayed slim. (His digestive problems and his "nervous stomach" were well known and much discussed; it's possible, indeed, that the friends and doctors who failed to pay attention to his complaints of failing health ascribed to hypochondria and even to hysteria what was a mortal condition.) There were those who called him "selfish, narcissistic, emotionally stunted, occasionally cruel." Yet the prevailing recollections of his acquaintances and friends attest to a sweetness of nature, a life-of-the-party brio and love of entertainment. All such accounts speak of his conviviality. If there was a piano in the room, he'd sit and improvise, then launch into a song. Music poured forth from Gershwin in full flood and at the slightest prompting: no hint of reticence here. The cultural avidity that marked his "habit of intensive listening" proved characteristic elsewhere also. His was a compulsion to perform.

It's hard to guess what would have happened had he pro-
gressed to middle or old age; there's a way in which the virtuoso
has, almost by necessity, a late-blooming emotional life. Maturation takes time. Like Carrington (though in his case of a glioblas-
toma, not gunshot) he died at thirty-eight. And given how much
of his time was spent by himself at the piano, he would have had
small chance to learn the lessons of accommodation most of us
acquire as we enter the workaday world. All those hours playing alone in practice rooms and then onstage to adoring applause
make egotism—or at least egocentricity—close to unavoidable. The standard interactions of the standard individual are not
within the prodigy's ken; he or she will fail to follow normal soci-
etal rules.

Friends and family urged Gershwin to get married, for example, and settle down with "a nice Jewish girl"; he preferred to
visit whorehouses and make love to other men's wives. His single
known child was illegitimate, a son born to a chorus girl—and
there are those who question the veracity of the claim by Alan
Gershwin (born Albert Schneider) that the composer was his father. As with any artist whose rise is meteoric, there are traces of
scorched earth in Gershwin's wake. To imagine him as an affable
elderly gentleman dandling grandchildren on his knee and teaching them to play "Chopsticks" on the Steinway in the family room
is to imagine a person he never became. Whether his sweetness
or his self-absorption would have predominated in the end is any-
body's guess.

A major new biography—a work by Richard Crawford now
more than thirty years in the making—remains to be published,

and Howard Pollack's excellent and comprehensive *George Gershwin: His Life and Work* (2006) is so evenhanded as to justify the arguments of yea- and naysayers alike. As Pollack writes, "Twentieth century depictions of Gershwin tended toward one of two scenarios. The first viewed him as a childlike genius who scaled the heights without benefit of formal instruction, a modest and somewhat naïve man scorned by disdainful critics and envious colleagues. The second regarded him, more darkly, as a flawed genius incapable of sustained study, but ambitious and vain and eager for critical approbation." The response to Gershwin's music mirrors the reaction to the human being; those who praise him, love him; those who dispraise, don't.

But whatever the truth or contradictory truths of this artist's personality, his achievement is indelible. And staggeringly large.

Here's a partial list of titles (roughly one for every forty) from the Gershwin songbook:

> "Bidin' My Time," "But Not For Me," "Do It Again," "Fascinating Rhythm," "A Foggy Day (In London Town)," "Funny Face," "Has Anyone Seen My Joe?," "How Long Has This Been Going On?," "Let's Call the Whole Thing Off," "Love Walked In," "The Man I Love," "'S Wonderful," "Shall We Dance," "Somebody Loves Me," "Someone to Watch Over Me," "They All Laughed," "They Can't Take That Away from Me," and "Wintergreen for President."

The chronology of Gershwin shows begins in 1919 — when he was not yet twenty-one — with *La La, Lucille*. That same season he wrote the music for the *Morris Gest Midnight Whirl*, and the next year *George White's Scandals of 1920*. In 1921 there was *A Dangerous Maid*, as well as that year's version of *Scandals*; in the subsequent three years he wrote *Our Nell, The Rainbow, Sweet Little Devil, Primrose,* and *Lady, Be Good*—and, not incidentally, *Rhapsody in Blue*. By the time of his death in 1938, the composer (working mostly but not exclusively with brother Ira as lyricist) had compiled an oeuvre both extensive and intensive; the sheer quantity—as well, of course, as quality—astonishes and daunts. From *Porgy and Bess* there are such classics as "My Man's Gone Now," "Bess, You Is My Woman Now," "It Ain't Necessarily So," "I Loves You, Porgy," "Oh Lawd, I'm on My Way," and—one of the most recorded songs in history—"Summertime." From the film made of *An American in Paris,* there are enduring numbers such as "Nice Work If You Can Get It," "Embraceable You," "I Got Rhythm," "Love Is Here to Stay," and "I'll Build a Stairway to Paradise." The piano rollography, for just the first six months of 1916, includes such player piano rolls as "Bring Along Your Dancing Shoes," "Kangaroo Hop," "You Can't Get Along with 'Em or Without 'Em," "At the Fountain of Youth," "Bantam Step," "When You're Dancing the Old Fashioned Waltz," "Honky Tonky (Down in Honky Tonky Town)," "Some Girls Do and Some Girls Don't," "And They Called It Dixieland," "When Verdi Plays The Hurdy-Gurdy," and "Oh Promise Me That You'll Come Back To Alabam'."

The list goes on. In performance after performance, it continues still today. As of this writing, both *Porgy and Bess* and the newly created retrospective *Nice Work If You Can Get It* have major engagements on Broadway, playing to sold-out houses. "When

Verdi Plays the Hurdy-Gurdy" gives some sense of the scope of this artist's endeavor; the highbrow and the lowbrow are "Dancing the Old Fashioned Waltz."

An aspect of "the art of youth" suggested, I hope, by the previous list is best summarized by a single word: "energy." *Energeia* seems a common denominator of the precocious or prodigious creative personality, and George Gershwin was nothing if not energetic; it's hard to fully apprehend how much he accomplished how fast. Working with a trainer, he valued physical stamina in his pursuits, and whether focused on a game of golf or Ping-Pong or tennis or weight lifting or dancing or boxing or painting or performing, he gave of himself unstintingly. *Exuberance* is part of this also; the candle burning at both ends stayed night after night brightly lit. As with Stephen Crane (though not so with Carrington, who was self-doubting and self-negating), one is struck by the abundance of the work produced.

Another word is "fluency." Gershwin's rate of composition rivals that of Baroque masters such as Telemann and Vivaldi, and there's a way in which his work for hire belongs to that tradition. Whether for a noble patron or the Church, much of the world's music has been written on commission—and this composer followed where his predecessors led. For his first orchestral project, the occasion was both public and commercial, an effort by a bandleader to educate as well as enlarge the audience for jazz. When Paul Whiteman invited the young artist (on the first of November 1923) to write a piece for an all-jazz concert he was planning to give in Aeolian Hall in New York City on February 12, 1924, Gershwin accepted with alacrity, then put the project aside.

"Legend has it that Gershwin forgot about the request until he read an article about the Whiteman concert in the *New York Herald Tribune* on 4th January which claimed that 'George Gershwin is at work on a jazz concerto, Irving Berlin is writing a syncopated tone poem and Victor Herbert is working on an American suite.'"

On January 7 he did commence to write, and the entirety of *Rhapsody in Blue* was produced in, roughly, three weeks. Even on opening night, the pianist improvised; on the score (transcribed for orchestra by Ferde Grofé) the piano solo is an extended cadenza indicated only by the marking: "Wait for nod." The soaring clarinet glissando of the opening motif was arrived at in rehearsal—in part as a joke proposed by Whiteman's clarinetist, Ross Gorman. Gershwin liked it and encouraged him, as it were, to wail away . . .

In this regard, at least, the label "jazz composer" does seem appropriate; by the end of 1927, Whiteman's band had performed the *Rhapsody* more than eighty times (its recording sold more than a million copies), and a kind of codification ensued. It made Gershwin rich. But to begin with, and certainly at its debut, the freewheeling score has the improvisational rush and bustle he had been proposing as America's characteristic syncopated rhythm; its music is the music of the streets. Gershwin claimed to have conceived the piece while riding a train to Boston and hearing "its steely rhythms, the rattle-ty-bang" of the tracks. Further, he remembered, "I heard it as a sort of musical kaleidoscope of America—of our vast melting pot, of our unduplicated national pep, of our metropolitan madness. By the time I reached Boston I had a definite plot of the piece, as distinguished from its actual substance."

The 1945 movie made of the composer's life, starring Robert Alda and with cameo appearances by, among others, Al Jolson and Paul Whiteman, is called *Rhapsody in Blue*—as though that opus represents his defining achievement. Oscar Levant appears as well, playing the music of his dead friend and reenacting their shared youth. Gershwin's story is fictionalized, romanticized, but does convey the feel and flavor of the period. Such descriptive phrases as "unduplicated national pep" and "our metropolitan madness" are bodied forth in black and white: all those highballs and high-kicking dancers, those willowy women and men in tuxedos who glide across the screen . . .

His first intention was to call the piece "American Rhapsody." At Ira's prompting he changed the title to emphasize its linkage to both jazz and the blues. (A parenthesis here: One cannot help but notice the crucial role in Gershwin's career played by his older brother. My assumption when discussing Crane was that the colleagues he met and admired in England would have kept him to the mark. And part of Carrington's diminishing productivity might derive from her increasing distance from other painters; her life with Strachey emphasized, instead, the written word. But the Gershwin brothers were unstinting in their admiration and support of each other, and their careers were, at least to begin with, coeval. Ira stood watch in the California hospital where his brother died. It's impossible to overstate the value of such partnership; "the art of youth"—no matter how individuated the achievement—has a collective aspect and profits from support.) In any case, his use of blue notes (generally, flatted third and seventh scale degrees, and sometimes flatted fifth degrees as well) and syncopated rhythms is now so broadly current as to seem traditional. Therefore we should remind ourselves of the composition's innovative daring; there had been nothing like it before.

The concertgoers knew this. Sergei Rachmaninov and Jascha Heifetz were in the crowd at Aeolian Hall; so were John Philip Sousa and the fifteen-year-old Elliott Carter. The audience roared its approval. The immediate reception of *Rhapsody in Blue* was sustained—indeed, rhapsodic—applause. But there were critical cavils and turned-up noses also; the composer Virgil Thomson, for example, wrote:

> In Gershwin's music the predominance of charm in presentation over expressive substance makes the result always a sort of *vers de société,* and his lack of understanding of all the major problems of form, of continuity, and of straightforward musical expression, is not surprising in view of the impurity of his musical sources and his frank acceptance of them.

And Olin Downes, reviewing the concert for the *New York Times* on February 13, 1924, took away with one hand what he offered with the other:

> [*Rhapsody in Blue*] shows extraordinary talent, just as it also shows a young composer with aims that go far beyond those of his ilk, struggling with a form of which he is far from being master . . . Often Mr. Gershwin's purpose is defeated by technical immaturity, but in spite of that . . . he has expressed himself in a significant, and on the whole, highly original manner.

Something had somehow happened that lifted the composer from creation of the ordinary—jazz and Dixieland and torch songs and dance tunes, no matter how inventive—to the extraordinary. It transpired at that moment in our history when the audience was ready to shift allegiance from the march-along music of the nineteenth century to the blues-tinged anthem of a new America. Through an alchemical process we recognize after the fact but can neither render formulaic nor by sheer will repeat, he was joining his own genius to the nation's genius. From "Alexander's Ragtime Band" to the blues of W. C. Handy, from klezmer music and the stride piano of Fats Waller to the jazz of Jelly Roll Morton, from Tin Pan Alley to the Cotton Club in Harlem, contemporary idioms were added to the crucible; the song-plugger performative aspects of Gershwin's early efforts became an original fusion and—to pursue the trope of alchemy—transmuted into gold. From the son of Russian immigrants, a new American art form emerged.

By November of 1924, putting on his other hat, Gershwin wrote *Lady, Be Good* (a musical revue starring Fred and Adele Astaire, with such songs as "Fascinating Rhythm" and "Leave It to Love") for Broadway. To have produced *Lady, Be Good* just ten months after *Rhapsody,* and with a clutch of individual hit melodies composed between, is emblematic of this artist's paired ambitions, and how they intertwined. He was making "joyful noise."

Here are some further testimonials. From the drama critic Alexander Woollcott:

> The first time I ever met George Gershwin, he came to dine with me at my hotel in Atlantic City. I saw before me a slim, swarthy, brilliant young man who, with his dark cheeks that could flood with color, his flashing smile and his marked per-

sonal radiance, did, when serving at the altar we call a piano, achieve a dazzling incandescence. But this was a mere dinner table, and his fires were banked, his light curtained in melancholy. He began by apologizing for the eccentric dinner he would have to order. 'You see,' he explained, 'I have terrible trouble with my stomach.'

Later I heard a great deal about Gershwin's stomach, and learned to understand its proper place in this thumb-nail sketch. Like you and me, Master Gershwin was profoundly interested in himself, but unlike most of us he had no habit of pretense. He was beyond, and to my notion, above, posing. He said exactly what he thought, without window dressing it to make an impression, favorable or otherwise. Any salient description of him must begin with this trait.

S. N. Behrman, a close friend, observes:

George's life was lived so out-of-doors, so in the public eye, and these activities so absorbed him that he was always 'too busy,' he said, for introspective agonies. He told me once that he wanted to write for young girls sitting on fire escapes on hot summer nights in New York and dreaming of love.

And Rouben Mamoulian (the director of the debut production of *Porgy and Bess*) writes:

George loved playing the piano for people and . . . at the slightest provocation. At any gathering of friends, if there was a piano on the room, George would play it . . . I know of no one who did it with such genuine delight and verve . . . He had a child's innocence and imagination. He could look at the same thing ever so many times and yet see it anew every time he looked at it and enjoy it . . . Yet at times he was like a patriarch.

I would look at him and all but see a long white beard and a staff in his hand . . . The simple gaiety of a child and the clear serenity of the old were two extremities of George's character. In between there was much of him that was neither simple nor clear, nor perhaps as happy. George did not live easily. He was a complicated, nervous product of our age.

These last observations ring true. Today the composer's music seems as quintessentially American as apple pie or baseball, but his musical contribution remains difficult to place. Is he the successful songwriter of some of his generation's most beloved popular music or an original genius whose fusion of jazz and classical music created a uniquely American musical synthesis? Gershwin wanted to be both. By and large the present verdict is that he succeeded, but while he lived—witness this chapter's epigraph—that verdict was less than unanimous, and he "did not live easily." Great fame brings great self-scrutiny, and he was always measuring the scope of his achievement (in terms of the size of his concert audience, the number of recordings sold, the applause at a performance); it rendered him "a complicated, nervous product of our age."

After the success of *Rhapsody,* Gershwin composed the Concerto in F. His score for *American in Paris* was in important ways balletic, and his groundbreaking *Porgy* was largely operatic. I will write of these projects hereafter, but the thing to notice now is that his "highbrow" efforts stood adjacent and not in opposition to his labors for the Broadway stage and, later, Hollywood. The symphonic mode, for Mozart, was not a violation of his work in chamber music or for solo instrument; the songs that Richard

Strauss composed did not negate his interest in tone poems or light opera; Johannes Brahms wrote for the human voice as well as sonatas for piano and cello. It's a question of *both-and,* not *either-or.* So it must have troubled Gershwin to be called unserious or, alternatively, pretentious—as though his success in the world of entertainment meant he should not trespass on the concert stage. Why not conjoin the two?

This seems to me a pivot point, a challenge that the artist chose to face. In his ear and his imagination, he was raising the stakes of the game. His first orchestral effort was either a laurel to rest on or a garland to conjoin with others, and he must have wondered if his training would suffice for formal composition. It would have been simple enough to say, *Thus far, no further,* and beat a more or less graceful retreat from the concert hall. ("I'm Sitting on Top of the World" was composed not by George Gershwin but by Ray Henderson, and the song was published in 1925. But Gershwin himself could rightfully claim to have attained, that year, that perch; he was sitting on top of the musical world and could well have toppled via a failure of balance. On July 20, 1925, his was the face on the cover of *Time,* and he had no need to prove himself again in the classical mode.) Yet as with any successful variation, Gershwin revisited the premise and enlarged upon the promise of what went before.

The writing of the concerto—originally titled "New York Concerto"—took an entire summer; the third movement was completed in late September 1925, at a friend's house in the village of Chautauqua, New York. It had been commissioned by the New York Symphony Orchestra at the suggestion of conductor

Walter Damrosch; the premiere took place (before the intermission Glazunov's Fifth Symphony and Rabaud's *Suite Anglaise* had been performed) on the afternoon of December 3. What emerged from Gershwin's first orchestral efforts—the *Rhapsody*, then the Concerto in F—is something very close to a revolution in sound.

It's tempting here to speculate on the composer's mental process, the moment when he recognized that *both-and* was in his reach and grasp. Now he commenced to style himself—and was acclaimed by others—as a "serious" artist, socializing with notables such as Stravinsky, Schoenberg, and Ravel. (At different times he had offered to serve as an apprentice to the even less formally tutored Irving Berlin, then Maurice Ravel and Nadia Boulanger; each turned him down, suggesting they had little of value to teach him and nothing he needed to learn.) Although at times he grumbled he was writing songs for money, not posterity, he took equal interest in each. More and more he thought about going to Europe to study counterpoint and the classical tradition. He valued both cash and cachet.

Gershwin's range and versatility would prove a model for composers such as Aaron Copland and Leonard Bernstein (who recorded *Rhapsody in Blue* with the New York Philharmonic in 1959). These artists in their separate ways incorporated colloquial idioms into our mandarin musical discourse, taking folk tunes or street vendor calls and making formal use of them; Charles Ives and Victor Herbert were doing much the same. Duke Ellington, the descendant of slaves, wrote music that proclaimed the rhythmic and melodic complexity of a new American mood. There are those who argue that the "great American composer" is in fact

Duke Ellington: that he more than any other figure of the period created a new dynamic and a new national song. Yet whatever will prove to be history's ranking and the hierarchy of achievement, Gershwin's writing constitutes a principal component of that innovative era. It stands the test of time. His songs and show tunes and operatic arias — with their syncopation, their intricate phrasing and key shifts — have become part of our musical heritage and central to the canon; their creator's reputation rests assured. As Virgil Thomson admitted (grudgingly, teeth-gnashingly): "Gershwin does not even know what an opera is; and yet *Porgy and Bess* is an opera and it has power and vigor. Hence it is a more important event in America's artistic life than anything American the Met has ever done . . ."

The composer wrote often and well about his own aspirations. Here, from "Our New National Anthem" (1925), is a representative passage:

> It is then as useless to deplore the triumph of jazz as it is to deplore the triumph of machinery. The thing to do is to domesticate both to our uses . . . It is for the trained musician who is also the creative artist to bring out this vitality and to heighten it with the eternal flame of beauty. When this time comes, and perhaps it is not so far away, jazz will be but one element in a great whole which will at last give a worthy musical expression to the spirit which is America. Meanwhile we can but do our best by writing what we feel and not what we think we ought to feel. And no one who knows America can doubt that jazz has its important place in the national consciousness.

Further, from "Fifty Years of American Music," (1929):

> For American music means to me something very specific,
> something very tangible. It is something indigenous, something
> autochthonous, something deeply rooted in our soul. It is mu-
> sic which must express the feverish tempo of American life. It
> must express the unique life we lead here—a life of weary ac-
> tivity—and our gropings and vain ideals. It must be a voice of
> the masses, a voice expressing our masses and at the same time
> immortalizing their strivings. In our music we must be able to
> catch a glimpse of our skyscrapers, to feel that overwhelming
> burst of energy which is bottled in our life, to hear that chaos
> of noises which suffuses the air of our modern American city.
> This, I feel, must be in every American music.
>
> And American music as such can hardly be said to be fifty
> years old. At most, it has been existing for only thirty years.

And in "The Composer in the Machine Age" (1930):

> Music is a phenomenon that to me has a very marked effect on
> the emotions. It can have various effects. It has the power of
> moving people to all of the various moods. Through the emo-
> tions, it can have a cleansing effect on the mind, a disturbing ef-
> fect, a drowsy effect, an exciting effect. I do not know to what
> extent it can finally become a part of the people. I do not think
> music as we know it now is indispensable although we have
> music all around us in some form or other. There is music in
> the wind.

· · ·

An artist's work resembles his or her own other work more closely
than that of anyone else; we leave our fingerprints all over every
page. A Picasso is a Picasso is a Picasso, no matter how change-

able the strategy deployed; his protean accomplishment could not be called by any other name. Yet what heralds the painter's career is at least in part variety; he would have endorsed Ralph Waldo Emerson's pronouncement that "a foolish consistency is the hobgoblin of small minds." Others disagree. Think of the distinction between Picasso and his early colleague in the exploration of cubism, Georges Braque. The former altered his brushwork and style repeatedly; the latter was persistent—refining, not redefining, his approach. These are two separate ways of being an artist, and it's beside the point to rank one above the other; some celebrate consistency, some don't.

In terms of this dichotomy also, George Gershwin tried for both. He was consciously a man who worked in different modes, but there's a through line in his music, whether show tune or concerto, dance score or opera. It's possible his early training as a song-plugger made him more accepting than would otherwise have been the case of borrowed bits of melody and snatches of overheard song. Yet to call him eclectic is, I think, inaccurate; this sort of borrowing and adaptation was nothing if not original. The composer collected taxi horns so as to make a sonorous cacophony of a city's traffic noise, and when he embarked upon *An American in Paris,* he amplified street sounds that were both familiar and strange. The third of his more formal efforts, *An American in Paris,* bears the same relation to the Concerto in F that the concerto bore to *Rhapsody in Blue;* it too is an attempt to alter the rules of the game.

In January 1928, he conceived an orchestral ballet; he had been to Paris two years before, and returned again in 1928, but seems to have been galvanized by the sight of the Hudson River (from his home on West 103rd Street in Manhattan). As he put it on a radio show in 1934:

> This piece describes an American's visit to the gay and beautiful city of Paris. We see him sauntering down the Champs-Élysées, walking stick in hand, tilted straw hat, drinking in the sights, and other things as well. We see the effect of the French wine, which makes him homesick for America. And that's where the blue begins, I mean the blues begin. He finally emerges from his stupor to realize once again that he is in the gay city of Pa-ree, listening to the taxi horns, the noise of the boulevards, and the music of the cancan, and thinking, "Home is swell! But after all, this is Paris — so let's go!"

*An American in Paris* has five sections, each with its own climax — the first two marked *"Con fuoco,"* the last three *"Grandioso."* The tourist passes buildings, meets a comely stranger — plausibly, a prostitute — and engages in musical dialogue (a solo violin and English horn) and escapes, it would appear, from the land of prohibition. There are short flute solos and dissonant leaps to suggest, if not inebriation, that Gershwin was, as he said of his visiting American, "drinking in the sights, and other things as well." As a narrative tone poem, there's something autobiographical and even confessional here. With its energetic melancholy and boulevardier's panache, it tells the tale of a decreasingly innocent abroad; words such as "debonair," "romantic," and "ironic" can serve as descriptors of the tonal range and mood.

He scored the piece "for piccolo, two flutes, two oboes, English horn, two clarinets, bass clarinet, two bassoons, alto, tenor, and baritone saxophones (all doubling on soprano saxophone), four horns, three trumpets, three trombones, tuba, timpani, percussion (snare drum, cymbal, bass drum, triangle, bells, xylophone, wood block, small and large tom-tom, and four taxi horns, each with its own pitch), celesta, and strings." There's a blaring brashness to this orchestration, and a jangling, tingling quasi-cacophony that poses a challenge for any conductor. Gershwin had promised the premiere performance, as a gesture of thanks for previous sponsorship, to Walter Damrosch; this took place at Carnegie Hall, with the New York Philharmonic-Symphony Society, on December 13, 1928. The reception of the piece was by and large ecstatic—although there were, as always, some cavils from the press. The composer appears to have preferred a version conducted by Fritz Reiner in Cincinnati on March 1, 1929; then his own conducting debut took place at Lewisohn Stadium in New York on August 29, 1929.

He pulled it off. From composer to soloist to conductor of his own compositions is a predictable journey, perhaps, but by no means inevitable. It took some daring for Gershwin to mount the podium for a full orchestra performance of his own demanding score. Nor would he be alone:

> *An American in Paris* subsequently became one of the most performed and recorded orchestral works of the twentieth century, with radio broadcasts and commercial releases conducted by Maurice Abravanel, Kenneth Alwyn, Leonard Bernstein, Ricardo Chailly, Carl Davis, Charles Dutoit, Arthur Fiedler, Lawrence Foster, Morton Gould, André Kostelanetz, Erich Kunzel, James Levine, Henry Lewis, Lorin Maazel, Neville Marriner, Wayne Marshall, Kurt Masur, Eduardo Mata, John Mauceri, Mitch Miller, Zubin Mehta, Eugene Ormandy, Seiji Ozawa, Libor Pesek, André Previn, Artur Rodzinski, Gunther Schuller,

Gerard Schwarz, Felix Slatkin, Leonard Slatkin, William Steinberg, Michael Tilson Thomas, Arturo Toscanini, and John Williams, among others.

The work gained an even larger audience in 1951, long after the composer's death. It became the central ballet of an MGM film directed by Vincente Minnelli, with a screenplay by Alan Jay Lerner and choreographed by—as well as starring—Gene Kelly, who partners with Leslie Caron. The producer, Arthur Freed, bought a series of songs from the Gershwin estate; Ira helped selecting and revising them, so the ballet turned into a kind of musical revue in the mode of the brothers' Broadway productions. The film was an instant success. Here it's useful to think of the contrast in America's national humor and mood; by the 1950s, the Great Depression was mere memory. When Gershwin wrote *An American in Paris,* his president soon would be Herbert Hoover, but the cinematic version came coincident with postwar prosperity and at the beginning of the Eisenhower years. The sense of loss that hovers near the center of the score was displaced by muscular enthusiasm (as represented by Gene Kelly) and the triumphal appearance of a lithe young man on the Champs-Élysées.

American soldiers landing in France are reputed to have shouted "Lafayette, we are here!" by way of returning the favor of military support; this movie was a Technicolor proclamation of a new conquering extravagance, if only in the tourist trade. *We have,* the trumpets seem to say, *arrived . . .*

• • •

George Gershwin surely had. He went on to compose the music for *East Is West* and *Show Girl* in 1929, *Girl Crazy* in 1930, *Delicious* and *Of Thee I Sing* in 1931, *George Gershwin's Song Book* the next year, and *Pardon My English* and *Let 'Em Eat Cake* in 1933. He wrote the *Second Rhapsody* in 1931, a draft of "Cuban Overture" in 1932, and *Variations on "I Got Rhythm"* in 1934. Not all of these were altogether successful, and none of the tunes surpassed the commercial yield of his first hit, "Swanee." Indeed, and to his consternation, *Let 'Em Eat Cake* and *Pardon My English* were flops in 1933, with fewer than one hundred performances apiece.

But the sheer bulk of composition, as suggested above, continues to astonish. His physical stamina, as well, continued unabated; in January and February 1934, he played twenty-eight concerts in twenty-eight days, barnstorming all over the country with the conductor Charles Previn and the Leo Reisman Orchestra. Night after night he played the Concerto in F, *Variations on "I Got Rhythm,"* *Rhapsody in Blue,* and a shifting selection of songs. It is as though he could scarcely keep pace with his teeming musical imagination—as though he wrote in some sort of self-imposed race against time, one eye on the metronome and one eye on the clock.

We must be careful here. It's tempting to imagine, when a major creative figure dies young, that she or he had premonitions of an early death and chose to work at speed. Retrospect is a great clarifier, and in retrospect it's clear Gershwin drove himself hard. But one could also argue that the act of composition was his single principal pleasure, and he delighted in the rush of production and always-imminent deadlines; the joie de vivre reported on by so many of his colleagues does not seem to include a sense of mortality approaching. Gloom and doom were not his style.

This points to a further distinction between the first acts of the composer and those of the writer and painter. Crane wrote, near his life's end, with a perhaps-embittered urgency and surely with a sense of waning strength. Carrington, by her life's final act, took the measure of art's solace and found it insufficient. But George Gershwin, it would seem, was felled by a "fell messenger" of whom he had scant warning; his death feels more akin to that of the soldier in battle or the victim of a crash. I mean by this that his demise was unexpected, not foretold or self-ordained, and we have to look at closure here as though it remains open-ended. For this particular artist, "the sense of an ending" was never in play, and in his case the art of youth remained a hopeful enterprise; it did not admit of decline.

The next of his great challenges came in a new arena. He had been given a copy of *Porgy*, the novel by DuBose Heyward, as long before as 1925; it took a full decade for the project to come to fruition on the Broadway stage. The story of the conception and then the composition and production of *Porgy and Bess* is well known; it's where Gershwin lays to rest the notion that "there are no second acts in American lives." By any measure of accomplishment, he was moving on.

The idea of writing an opera had been with him for some time. In 1929 (the year he contemplated working on *The Dybbuk* for the Metropolitan Opera Company) he told Isaac Goldberg:

I'd rather make my own mistakes—break my own paths. I've been thinking for a long time of an operatic book involving the mixed population of our country. New York is not only an American city; it is a meeting place, a rendezvous of the nations. I'd like to catch the rhythms of these interfusing peoples,—to show them clashing and blending. I'd like especially to blend the humor of it with the tragedy of it. Temperamentally I cannot enter with full sympathy into the exploitation of glorified "mushy" themes. I recognize, of course, that the highest musical expression must consider the ecstasies: but all heart and no head produce a soft, fibreless sort of music. I should want in however grand an opera, to find the head well in control of the heart.

And so, whatever else I may produce in the way of a serious opera, I shall not be content until I have managed to experiment satisfactorily with a libretto free of the conventional sentimentality that makes even the noble heroines and heroes secretly ridiculous to the very crowds that applaud them.

For a song-plugger turned songwriter and composer, the writing of an opera would seem a more or less natural progression. His stock-in-trade, one could argue, had been both recitative and tuneful melody since he began to compose. From the conventions of the music hall and nightclub to the conventions of the opera is a step but not a leap; why not write an aria for the classically trained voice? "A rendezvous of the nations," as Gershwin describes "the mixed population of our country," lends itself to precisely the kind of hybrid theatrical endeavor that opera consists of and that he'd engaged in for years.

It's a daunting prospect nevertheless, and perhaps particularly so if the tyro is American. To hail from Vienna or Rome is to come from a tradition of operatic excellence, a culture long steeped in the form. But a composer born in Brooklyn has no such history of sustained appreciation for this particular musical mode, and Gershwin was in any case anxious to "make my own mistakes—break my own paths." When finally he plunged headlong into the writing of *Porgy and Bess,* it was with his typical near-total concentration, but the "overture" took time. And once he committed himself, he found he had embarked upon a very large project indeed. Larry Starr puts it well:

> As the Brooklyn-born son of an immigrant Jewish couple from Russia, Gershwin was an aggressive assimilationist. He desired above all to become a quintessential American and to be regarded, nationally and internationally, as a musical spokesman for his country . . . Living in a society and at a time burdened with longstanding and painful issues centering upon race, Gershwin created music in which "white" and "black" influences coexist in evocative but reassuring harmony. It seems no mere accident that the magnum opus of this self-consciously modern, unabashedly urban, wealthy, white, northern assimilationist is a work that celebrates the story of a "backward," segregated, lower-class community of Gullah blacks in Charleston, South Carolina.

The aristocratic DuBose Heyward had lived most of his life in Charleston and knew the world of "Goat Sammy"—a crippled half-crazed beggar whom he portrayed as the heroic Porgy—intimately. His novel *Porgy* became a best seller in 1925 and two years later had a successful run on Broadway as a play of the same name. Gershwin read the book and saw the play and evidently ruminated early on as to the possibility of setting it to music; the two men met, then corresponded at length. A deal of temporizing ensued, with conflicting schedules and prior commitments (Al Jolson, together with Jerome Kern and Oscar Hammerstein II, would obtain and then release the rights for production), while Gershwin continued to wrestle with the problem of how best to write an opera. It was a new kind of challenge for him; his knowledge of the world of poor southern blacks on "Catfish Row" was next to nonexistent, and he ran the risk of stereotype and re-creating Uncle Tom; Duke Ellington himself would criticize the work in terms of its "lampblack Negroisms." For a man whose first success had been derivative of minstrelsy, with Al Jolson wearing blackface, there were obstacles abounding in the wings.

But Gershwin rose to the occasion and—though there are those who disagree—more than met the challenge. One way to measure artistic growth is to compare the melody of "Swanee" with what he composed for *Porgy and Bess;* the music of the latter outstrips the former both in terms of originality and authenticity. The composer spent time with Heyward and his wife in Charleston and on Folly Island; he steeped himself in Negro spirituals, the call-and-response of prayer chants, the music of the streets.

For Gershwin, this immersion in black southern life seemed "more like a homecoming than an exploration," according to Heyward, who recalled that one night "at a Negro meeting on a remote sea-island, George started 'shouting' with them, and eventually to their huge delight stole the show from their champion 'shouter.'"

Without dwelling overmuch on this, it's possible to link the world of Gullah blacks and shtetl, if not ghetto, Jews; there's an affinity here. One has the sense of an artist alert to stimuli, immersed in something new to him that was to others familiar. Gershwin responded to the music made by black men and women singing in church with a bone-deep sympathy; he had long admired jazz musicians up in Harlem, but Gullah chanting struck new chords. The northward journey Porgy undertakes (on the trail of Bess and Sportin' Life) is a cross between "the great migration" and the immigrant experience; when he calls New York "the promised land," it's hard not to think of the composer exalting the metropolis, though with more than a touch of melancholy, since Porgy won't likely succeed.

Too, the conventions of musical theater lend themselves to the opera stage, and choral work is central to the opera's conception. When he doubled the number of titular characters, adding Bess to Porgy (Bess has no self-engendered solo in the libretto), he gave himself the chance to write, as well as arias, duets. Part of this derives, I think, from the fruitful opposition of Gershwin and Heyward themselves; theirs is a classic instance of thesis and antithesis or the way that opposites attract.

In Heyward as collaborator, Gershwin found almost the perfect partner for realizing in musical-theatrical terms this story about the crippled beggar Porgy and the poor blacks of Charleston. Where Gershwin was the bumptious, quick-moving, quicktalking New Yorker, Heyward was introverted, courtly, and reserved, slowed down and physically impeded by the aftereffects of a crippling attack of polio suffered in his youth. Moreover, in contrast to Gershwin's somewhat rootless Russian-Jewish, newimmigrant background, Heyward was a Southern aristocrat of plantation-owner stock. He could trace his lineage to Thomas Heyward, one of the signers of the Declaration of Independence.

Heyward and Ira wrote the lyrics, dividing the responsibility and collaborating on a few songs such as "I Got Plenty o' Nuttin," "Bess, You Is My Woman Now," and "I Loves You, Porgy." Generally, Gershwin set his new partner's words to music and gave his brother melodies to versify. At first Heyward wanted spoken dialogue, but the composer insisted on recitative. He insisted also that the opera be cast with African American performers rather than white performers in blackface, the common practice. Because this last stipulation made it implausible to mount the production at the Met, *Porgy and Bess* premiered on Broadway on October 10, 1935. (On balance, this proved preferable for the show's creators; it meant they did not have to rotate in and out of a repertory cycle. But it has much to do with why the theater-going public thinks of *Porgy* as musical theater rather than pure opera.) "With Paul Robeson away in Europe for most of 1934–35, Gershwin settled instead on Todd Duncan, who had performed in New York productions like *Cavalleria Rusticana*, taught at Howard University, and initially scorned the idea of playing the original Porgy as something smacking of Tin Pan Alley and beneath him. Gershwin persisted, however, and Duncan rejoiced that he did. 'I literally wept for what this Jew was able to express for the Negro,' he told the composer Ned Rorem and particularly cited his final song 'I'm on My Way' as moving him to tears."

The literature on *Porgy and Bess* is immense and needs no elaboration. Suffice it to say that the debut performance was greeted with thunderous applause; the Gershwins and Heyward joined the cast for seven curtain calls. "This is the sort of thing that Pulitzer Prizes are not good enough for," wrote Arthur Pollock in the *Brooklyn Daily Eagle*. And though there were and are complaints about cultural imperialism—the arrogant arrogation of other people's musical traditions, the stereotyping of black behavior—*Porgy* seems to me an inspired effort and one, three-quarters of a century later, that continues to enthrall. When I saw and heard Audra McDonald in the role of Bess last season, I felt as though an American icon were blood and flesh incarnate, brought blazingly to life. What she and the other cast members offered up eight times a week is full-throated celebration, a story turned triumphantly to song. If *The Red Badge of Courage* is Stephen Crane's signature achievement, this "folk opera" is Gershwin's: an innovative enterprise that has not been equaled since. It's as though he understood that what he there and then composed was writ not in water but stone.

The final labors were indeterminate, a kind of intermission. After the effort of *Porgy and Bess,* it was as though he needed a respite, though he took no sort of rest. The world of Broadway was contracting, the world of the movies expanding, and many premiere artists traveled west. In August of 1936, George and Ira left for an extended sojourn in Hollywood to write music and lyrics for what would become three films. The first of these, initially titled "Watch Your Step," then "Stepping Toes," became *Shall We Dance*—a score that as the names suggest was written for a dance team, the debonair Fred Astaire and his partner Ginger Rogers (with whom Gershwin had a brief fling). Exasperated by the delays and demands of studio conditions, the composer nonetheless produced some of his loveliest melodies, including "They Can't

Take That Away from Me" (which was nominated for but did not win the Academy Award for Best Original Song in 1937). The musical also included "They All Laughed" and "Let's Call the Whole Thing Off."

It's convenient to deploy these titular assertions, for one has the sense that Gershwin and Hollywood were less than perfect partners; his employers harbored some suspicion of his "highbrow" aspirations as a result of *Porgy*. What they wanted from him was entertainment sufficiently broad to make certain that "They All Laughed," and he was more than a little tempted to "Call the Whole Thing Off." When he spoke of Samuel Goldwyn as "Goldwyn the Great," he did not intend a compliment. Writing to his sister Frankie that year, he confessed, "I don't think I've scratched the surface. I'm out here to make enough money with movies so that I don't have to think about money anymore. Because I just want to work on American music: symphonies, chamber music, opera. That is what I really want to do."

Despite his commercial commitments, he was making plans for another opera and began composing a string quartet in his head. He thought, as well, of writing a symphony; he spent time with Arnold Schoenberg, an unlikely-seeming companion who — while playing tennis or sitting for a portrait — helped hone his "classical" aspirations. Gershwin's friend Verna Arvey further reported that he planned to write "a composition for orchestra and chorus about Abraham Lincoln, about whom he had thought and read much."

None of these plans came to fruition, and it's hard to know how seriously he took them or how much time he spent on "what I really want to do." He was exercising and swimming and, at his trainer's urging, taking hikes in the hills; at night he was living the high life in the homes of movie moguls or hosting parties in an extravagant house he and Ira and Ira's wife, Leonore, rented in Beverly Hills. Seemingly—although more easily for Ira, who would remain in California—the Gershwins settled down. The composer fell in love *seriatim* with starlets and decisively with (Charlie Chaplin's secret wife) Paulette Goddard. More and more he spoke of marriage, but she was out of bounds.

The history of Hollywood has many such episodes of mismatched aspirations: artists gone west for the money and comfort, then finding out, in Wordsworth's phrase, that "getting and spending, we lay waste our powers." Gershwin had traveled an almost unimaginable distance from his first homes in Brooklyn and the Lower East Side; his behavior also changed. The enthusiastic innocence and wide-eyed enthusiasm so widely attested to by those who knew him earlier now somehow began to seem spoiled. He grew short-tempered, irritable, even irrational—trying to push people out of cars, shouting at old friends for no apparent reason. It's probable the transformation of his personality was a function of the tumor's growth; he could settle down to work only when the headaches were not blinding. His sister-in-law, Leonore, however, believed he was playacting in order to gain sympathetic attention; when he fumbled with his cutlery or stumbled and fell to the pavement, she told him to grow up. Modern medicine could perhaps resolve (and might have furnished a solution to) what were in those days riddles; to paraphrase one of his titles, "how long had this been going on," and could it have been stopped?

In any case, and in short order, the brothers wrote *A Damsel in Distress*—again for Fred Astaire, though this time with Joan Fontaine. This score includes such classics as "A Foggy Day" and "Nice Work If You Can Get It." They also planned a series of songs for *The Goldwyn Follies,* a lavish musical revue. But while conducting the Los Angeles Philharmonic in a rehearsal in February of 1937, Gershwin lost his balance and nearly fell from the podium. A few nights later, while performing *An American in Paris,* he found it difficult to control his hands and was seized with an incapacitating headache. Doctors could find no physical cause for his symptoms, which—after a battery of tests—were attributed to overwork and then hysteria. He was sent home to rest.

The headaches and the vertigo continued. He told his childhood friend Yip Harburg that a brain tumor had been ruled out; he told his mother, Rosa, not to fly west to tend him but to remain on the East Coast. All his life he'd worried loudly about his delicate digestive tract; now, facing mortal illness, he stayed largely stoic—even silent. Till the very end Leonore and others believed he was dissembling and would get better soon. There would be, however, neither a happy ending nor any reversal of fortune in the stock Hollywood fashion; things went from bad to worse.

Here's a bare-bones summary of the curtain call. On the evening of July 9, 1937, George Gershwin collapsed and lapsed into a coma; he was rushed to Cedars of Lebanon Hospital, where he was at long last diagnosed with a brain tumor. There were frantic efforts to secure the most accomplished surgeons and neurologists; special planes were commandeered for transcontinental flights. A medical team assembled and did what then seemed possible, but the patient never regained consciousness. On July 11, 1937, at the age of thirty-eight, and after a five-hour operation, the composer died.

The mourning was national, even international; funeral services were held simultaneously on July 15 at Temple Emanu-El in Manhattan and Temple B'nai B'rith (now renamed the Wilshire Boulevard Temple) in Los Angeles. The honorary pallbearers included the governor of New York State, Herbert H. Lehman, and New York City's mayor, Fiorello La Guardia; the music played at the service included selections from Bach, Beethoven, Handel, and Schumann.

At the ceremony in Manhattan, Rabbi Stephen S. Wise said in part, "There are countries in Central Europe which would have flung out this Jew. America welcomed him and he repaid America by singing the songs of America's soul with the gusto of a child, with a filial tenderness of a son." George Gershwin was buried in a family plot in Mount Hope Cemetery, Hastings-on-Hudson; his mother converted it shortly thereafter into a mausoleum.

On August 9, a record crowd of more than twenty thousand people assembled in Lewisohn Stadium for a memorial concert; roughly twenty-six thousand people attended a concert one month later (September 8, 1937) at the Hollywood Bowl—this one broadcast live around the world. Otto Klemperer led the Los Angeles Philharmonic in an orchestral transcription of the second of the Three Preludes for piano; Fred Astaire, George Jessel, Al Jolson, and Oscar Levant were among those taking part in the event. The national outpouring of grief rivals the mourning at funerals for presidents and major movie stars; the eulogies were numerous, stressing the size of the loss. In a memorial tribute,

Arnold Schoenberg called his friend "a great composer" whose music was not only "to the benefit of a national American music" but also "a contribution to the music of the whole world." That verdict stands.

What, therefore, may we make of this third of our trio of artists, the one whose impact during his lifetime was largest and who died at or near the apogee of fame? Any study of the composer's career must properly focus on his achievement—yet I want to stress, in summary, the size of his ambition. Stephen Crane could be self-deprecating and dismissive of his own work; Carrington was plagued by doubt and destroyed a large proportion of her art. But George Gershwin represents the creative personality who does not take no for an answer, who displays an almost limitless assurance the brass ring is his to grasp. There was nothing that he would not try, no commission he refused or dare he would not take.

It's worth remembering how many of our entertainers—particularly, perhaps, our musicians—die young. These are performers more importantly than composers (the reverse of Gershwin's case), and most of them had not been born when our subject died. But think, in the last decades, of Duane Allman, Mama Cass, Kurt Cobain, Sam Cooke, Buddy Holly, Janis Joplin, Jimi Hendrix, Jim Morrison, Charlie Parker, Otis Redding, Amy Winehouse, and the rest. A career in the limelight has always had risks—more than ever, perhaps, in the "flame-out" modern moment—and self-destructiveness can look, at times, like the flip side of the coin of creation. Yet one does not have the sense, with this artist, of talent squandered or misspent. What killed Gershwin was neither recklessness nor self-abuse, neither drink nor drugs nor a plane crash nor tractor accident nor shotgun; he took careful care of himself. Nonetheless, death came for him—as for those I've named above—before the age of forty; it almost seems a by-blow of the trade.

One of his female friends, Kitty Carlisle Hart, recollects:

> George was so dear. He had everything, but there was something terribly vulnerable about him. People felt very protective about him. Why I don't know. He was successful, he was good-looking, women adored him, he had money. He had everything, but yet there was something vulnerable, childlike. He needed approval. Yes, maybe that's it. And you felt it. That was part of his charm. Enthusiasm—that was part of his charm too. And his enthusiasm was terribly boyish for a man who was that successful. He had an enormous sense of enjoyment and enthusiasm which he infused into everything he did. And enormous energy, and there's nothing quite as sexy as energy, is there? What else is there?

She was born twelve years after Gershwin and died a full seventy later, at the age of ninety-six, in 2007. He may once have proposed to her; he surely propositioned her, but she married Moss Hart instead. I cite Ms. Hart at chapter's close because her lengthy closing acts (the decades of appearances on *To Tell the Truth* and at charity balls, the cabaret performances and omnipresence at social events, the twenty years as chair of the New York State Council on the Arts, etc.) attest to her power of self-preservation and the staying power of charm. What Kitty Carlisle remembers of Gershwin—his enthusiasm, his energy—are signature compo-

nents of the elderly woman and the young man alike; these quali-
ties exist outside of time.

That, at any rate, is the argument I made in *Lastingness: The Art
of Old Age.* In my study of musicians, writers, and painters who
advance their art past the age of seventy, the common denominator is "energy," an attribute of character that somehow does
survive. It's clear that Gershwin had it, clear he did not lose it,
unlikely that he would have done so in the years to come. No artist—and certainly no critic or biographer—can predict the unknown future's yield; my best guess is, however, he would have
continued to grow.

Hart's fond description's other term, "enthusiasm," derives
from the Greek *"en theos,"* the arrival of the penetrating god. The
inexact but evocative phrase "life force" is part of this too. The
élan vital in Gershwin is attested to by everyone who joined him
on the dance floor or listened to him improvise at three thirty in
the morning or watched him at the keyboard or conductor's podium. His seems an exemplary instance of a musician invaded by
music, and the electric force of it—*en theos*—was with him all his
life. Such forcefulness does not falter or ebb; it can, however, die.

The septuagenarian A. E. Housman wrote, early on, in "To
an Athlete Dying Young," of the ephemeral nature of triumph:
"Smart lad, to slip betimes away / From fields where glory does
not stay." In a subsequent couplet he asserts, "Now you will not
swell the rout / Of lads that wore their honours out."

Yet Gershwin's glory and honor have, if anything, increased.
Our culture is in important ways enriched by his inventiveness;
his songs and his "folk opera" and orchestral compositions are

omnipresent still. Jacob Gershvin continues to move us; his glad, sad, haunting melodies are part of the national song. On radio stations, in cabarets and concert halls and nightclubs, on college campuses and summer stock platforms, around the pianos in private homes where friends share sheet music and gather to sing—in venue after venue his work thrives.

This third of our three subjects is the clearest example of a growth pattern cancelled by premature death. His was an unyielding certainty that music is what crucially counts, and there's nothing to suggest a weakening of that conviction in his final days. The questions with which this chapter begins—*what if, what else, what next?*—must remain unanswered, but the art of youth is here embodied, its soaring ambition achieved.

# 5

## The Beginner

When I was one-and-twenty
I heard a wise man say,
"Give crowns and pounds and guineas
But not your heart away;
Give pearls away and rubies
But keep your fancy free . . ."

— A. E. HOUSMAN

THIS BOOK HAS DEALT with three separate modes of creative expression: music, painting, and literature. Of these three, it seems to me, talent shows itself the latest in the last. The vocabulary of music is wordless and therefore universal; those with unfettered access to it seem to have gained that access in the crib. Visual acuity declares itself quickly as well; a sensitivity to line and color is established early on. Yet there's a difference between childhood speech and *The Decameron* or *Madame Bovary*; those works could not have been composed by a four- or six-year-old. Experience digested or imagined is the lifeblood of literature, and none of us are born with an instructed eloquence. The woman or man whose art form is verbal must acquire fluency syllable by syllable; all authors hone their craft.

There *are* examples of prowess in youth; we need only name Arthur Rimbaud and Percy Bysshe Shelley—or our previous subject, Stephen Crane—to celebrate early achievement. A number of poets and some prose writers and playwrights do their important work young. By comparison with the roster of composers and visual artists, however, the list of writers who attain creative mastery at career's start is short; mostly it's a learning curve and, with luck, an upward arc. In this chapter, I will use my own experience of that learning curve—not, of course, to place myself even by adjacency in the company of those excellent artists I've discussed but because all adults once were beginners themselves. In a book of brief biographies a brief autobiographical essay may enlarge upon the notion of first acts.

We all invent our pasts. I cannot remember the moment when I began to speak and cannot remember the moment at which I decided to write. Rather, and naturally, the whole is a continuum. It is a series of moments and set of lines crossed that appear far clearer in retrospect than they ever did in prospect. To take one such example, I do remember learning how to read. I had just turned six years old and was with my family on the SS *Queen Mary,* crossing from Southampton to New York. On the third day of the voyage out—having passed some watermark that meant we were closer to America—I received my first pair of long pants. And that afternoon (sitting cross-legged on the stateroom floor, so proud of my flannels I hated to crease them, the sun through the porthole spotlighting the letters) I taught myself to read. It was a book about boats. There was a lighthouse, a bridge, a series of ships—from trireme to frigate, canoe to destroyer, with two whole pages devoted to the fireboats, their spray a white, wet arc.

The captions distinguished between them; so could I. The alphabet's tumblers went "click." I remember the feel of it, the pride in it, the pleasure, the way the world made sense. I think I remember telling my father I had no time for shuffleboard; I know I took the book up to the deck for tea. It was wonderful: the way the lines pictured this life I was leading. Everything signified; everything fit. Our steward was called Jonathan; I recognized his badge as his spelled name. The rest of the trip is a jumble, but this sudden perception of order—the deck chairs ranked in rows like language, how a page is organized and why you turn it when—remains indelible. I learned to read that day.

Many years later, however, I was sorting through some papers in the attic of my father's house. He was moving one last time, and I had come to help discard the past's detritus. In a box full of grade-school report cards, letters home from camp, and other such accumulation, I came across a book titled *Henry's Green Wagon*. It was familiar, faintly; it conjured up Great Britain, not the United States. The boy on the disintegrating cover was pink-cheeked and wearing blue shorts. I read the inscription. "To Master Nicky Delbanco," it said. "The best reader in Miss Jamaiker's Kindergarten Class. Congratulations. First Prize."

Miss Jamaiker's was the school across the street. Like any other English child, I had been taught to read *before* the age of six. So the memory is false. It is clear but confused. Although I remember the school, the vast-seeming meadow I would traverse on the way home, the hedgehog's lair, the way my aunt would shepherd us, a clearing in the woods that I called Hansel's house—though I remember much of this I had forgotten I knew how to read. There are explanations. Probably I learned in stages. Maybe I faked it with *Henry's Green Wagon,* having memorized the book and turning the pages when it seemed proper to turn. That sunshot moment on the *Queen Mary* may have illuminated something else instead. The transatlantic crossing was a rite of passage, after all, and what I learned while sitting on the deck chair may not have been the alphabet. Therefore, the critic's question: How accurate are such accounts?

I'm told I was a quiet child and then a burbling, noisy one. I remember making speeches—for birthday parties and the like—in rhyme: *Happy birthday to you; sappy worth day to who?* Or *For he's a jolly good fellow, for she prefers orange to yellow.* The grownups would sit and applaud while I declaimed my doggerel, and only later did I recognize how much of their praise was indulgent. When Bob blows his tin trumpet or Babs does a pirouette, it's something to enjoy, perhaps, but not a prodigy's attainment; it's children announcing their place in the world. When Dick has learned his alphabet or Jane begins to read aloud, it's cause for celebration but not awe.

At the time I thought that coupling "June" with "spoon" and "moon" was proof of my inventiveness, clear evidence that I'd been singled out. Now, decades later, I can see this might have been predictive of a life lived in language—though not, of course, of anything prodigious or astonishing. Alexander Pope's "An Essay on Criticism" (1711) appeared when he was twenty-three and was composed two years before; it includes the phrase "a little learning is a dang'rous thing," but by then he knew—and knew them well—Italian, French, Latin and Greek. *I* had a little learning, and enough to know I wanted more, but that's a very different thing than remarkable skill to start with. An uncle called me *"Quatschkopf,"* or "nonsense-head" and chatterbox; he was right.

So Little Jack Horner and Little Miss Muffet and the rest of the creatures from Mother Goose were my visitors each morning; later, I recited Alfred Noyes and Alfred, Lord Tennyson, until I fell asleep. Humpty-Dumpty had a different metrical pattern than did "Hiawatha"; I matched my skip steps to them on the way to school. Poetry, it seems to me, is easier of access than prose fiction (by "poetry" I mean here the sonorous din of nursery rhyme), and the genre with which most young writers begin. I cannot remember a time, in truth, when words were not my silent companions and some sort of patter was not in my head; the sound and look of English compelled me from the start. There are children who respond to melody or contour with a quickened pulse and full attention; my siren song was speech.

Then, at the age of ten, I fell ill, with the rheumatic fever for which, at the time, bed rest was prescribed. Penicillin too was part of the cure, and no doubt more effective: a pink liquid I swallowed twice daily when carried to the bathroom by my mother or a nurse. This happened many years ago; I'm fine; that raspberry-flavored concoction did its restorative work. But looking back, I think those months of lying in bed with nothing to stave off my boredom but books were formative; the Hardy Boys, Chip Hilton, the Knights of the Round Table, the soldiers of the Civil War all kept me company and kept imagination active while motion was enjoined. By the time I grew mobile again I'd acquired the habit of reading—and the chance later on to lie in a hammock and read *War and Peace* or *Bleak House* or *The Charterhouse of Parma* seemed somehow to partake of the process of recovery; I turned the corner back to health by turning page after page.

(Parenthetically, this seems to me a more-than-personal history or private compensation. A surprisingly large number of artists report on something similar: an enforced inactivity during childhood while their fancy roamed. Alexander Pope, for instance, contracted an illness when young—Pott's disease, it now appears—and was deformed as well as growth-stunted thereafter. But writer after writer tells of having discovered a vocation while lying on the couch or bed and leafing through a book. How else escape the confines of a world walled in by pillows; how else enlarge experience when chair- or wheelchair-bound?)

The child who keeps a diary or outlines a comic book adventure—full of monsters and spaceships and dungeons—is practicing her or his craft. So is the one with a coloring book who fills in the outlines of clouds. A majority of such practitioners will at some point grow self-conscious or aware of limitation and put away childish things. The ukulele ends up in a yard sale; the diaries get packed away or burned. I sometimes wonder if the yearning desire to write a book or paint when elderly is a return to that unfettered period when language was not scrutinized or perspective subject to correction—if the eighty-year-old who dictates her life story or joins a watercolor class is trying to recapture what was relinquished when young. The pleasures of expressiveness are widespread in our early years, when art—which Freud defined as "socially validated daydreaming"—appears accessible.

The mystery is why, for some, the path of access opens out and why for others shuts down.

I have been the full-fledged student of a writer only once. John Updike was, I think, one of the most literate and able critics of our time. His breadth of reading, acuity of insight, and grace of expression would give most scholars pause; he would no doubt have been welcomed at any institution in the fifty states. But he remained at a stiff arm's remove from academe, earning his living by the pen alone. In 1962, however, his resolution wavered and he agreed to teach—at Harvard Summer School. I wanted to remain in Cambridge and therefore applied for the course. It was an offhand decision; I barely had heard (more excusable in those years) of his name. When he accepted me into his fiction workshop, it would have been ungrateful to drop out.

In retrospect I see more clearly how lucky and right was that choice. The first word I wrote for Updike was the first of my first novel. Like every other self-respecting undergraduate, I planned to be either a poet, folk singer, or movie star. I considered "prose" and "prosaic" to be cognate terms. (They are, admittedly, but I know something more by now about the other three professions and would not trade.) The young man's fancy is poetic, and his models are Rimbaud or Keats. Mine were, at any rate; my first compositions were suicide notes. But I was signed up for a prose-writing workshop with no idea of what to write and not much time to decide. The day of that decision is vivid to me still.

A friend and I were strolling around a lake in Wellesley; we'd been reading for final exams. I heard him out as to his future; then he had to listen to me. I had tried my hand already at the shorter stuff, I said; I was going to write a novel. That was what a summer should consist of — something ambitious, no piddling little enterprise like Chekhov's but something on the scale of, let's say, *Moby-Dick*. Yet before I wrote my masterpiece, I had to plan it out. What do first novels consist of, I asked — then answered, nodding sagely at a red-haired girl in a bikini emerging from the lake. First novels are either the myth of Narcissus or the parable of the Prodigal Son — but generally disguised, and often unwittingly so. Their authors do not understand they fit an ancient mold. I already knew enough about Narcissus, I announced, and therefore would elect the latter; I'd rewrite the parable. The difference was that my revision would be conscious — whereas most young novelists fail to see themselves in sufficiently explicit mythic terms.

That was not my problem, but there were problems to solve. I knew nothing about the landscape of the Bible, for instance, and needed a substitute. My friend lit a cigarette; we considered. It happened that I'd been to Greece the previous summer and traveled wide-eyed for weeks. I would replace one location with the other. The parable has three component parts: the son leaves home, spends time away, and returns. My novel too would have three components, with Rhodes and Athens as its locales. My Greek protagonist would go from the island to the city and — in a phrase from the parable itself — "eat up his substance with whores."

The girl in the bikini trailed drops of water where she walked; she shook her long hair free. I instructed my friend that *hetarae* — the Greek word for courtesans — had "Follow Me" incised backward on their sandals so they could print enticements and directions in the dust. She rounded a bend in the path. The question of contemporaneity engaged me for three minutes. I knew enough about modern-day Greece to fake it, possibly, but knew I'd never know enough about the ways of antique Attica; the prostitute's sandal exhausted my lore. It would take less research to update the story. So there, within fifteen minutes, I had it: a contemporary version of the parable of the Prodigal Son that followed the text faithfully and yet took place in Greece. The rest was an issue of filling in blanks; I started to, next week.

I have told this tongue-in-cheek, but it is nonetheless true. The epigraph of my first novel is the first line of the parable; the great original is buried in my version, phrase by phrase. I revised *The Martlet's Tale* many times and by the time I'd finished was no longer a beginner. Looking back, I'm astonished, however; it all fell so neatly in place. An editor at J. B. Lippincott ushered me into his office and said they were honored to bring out the book. "You're a very fortunate young man," he said, but I thought his politeness routine. I took success for granted when it came. My photograph in magazines seemed merely an occasion for judging the likeness; a long and flattering review in the *New York Times* on publication day was no more than an author expected; I ate expensive lunches with the cheerful certainty that someone else would pay.

In some degree, moreover, this very blindness worked to my advantage. I had been accustomed to a schoolboy's notion of success. I would have dealt with failure far less equably. Had Updike not encouraged me, I cannot say for certain if I would have persevered; there were many wind-scraps in the wind, and I followed the favoring breeze. Harvard does prepare you for the world in this one crucial way: if you succeed within those walls, you assume that you will when outside. When I handed in the first pages of *The Martlet's Tale* and my professor's reaction was praise, I concluded that the rest must follow as the night does day. I suppose I stood out in his class; I certainly tried to; his wary approval meant much. I wrote a second chapter and was hooked.

Paragraphs three through six of this chapter—as well as the description, above, of starting to write my first novel—are lines I have published before. In *Group Portrait: Conrad, Crane, Ford, James & Wells* (1982) I composed a biographical study of writers in community, and the screen memory of learning to read is embedded in that text. The recollection of John Updike comes from an autobiographical essay I published in 1985 and modified for a book of "reflections on the literary life," *The Lost Suitcase* (2000). It would have been easy, of course, to rewrite those passages, but I decided to leave well enough alone. I confess this not because I fear the charge of plagiarism or copyright infringement—it's my own language, after all—but because it seems to me that repetition haunts us, particularly as we age. The formulaic anecdote or story repeated verbatim grows almost unavoidable in an older person's speech. There's the familiarity of habit, the comfort of the twice-told tale.

Not so for youth. Under the sun, all is new. Conception—that great word of art and life—is various, and each apprentice maker must invent the wheel. Those wheels have been rolling since time out of mind, yet every time we start, we start afresh. Or at least it *feels* that way; we tell ourselves that what we're doing has never before been done. Every dawn is rosy-fingered and every full moon ripe with possibility; each line inscribed on the etching plate or page or score is there for the first time. "When I close my eyes, it's night," as the woman in the adage says; there's a solipsistic conviction, on the artist's part, that nothing was or is or will be quite the same.

*Enemies of Promise,* a book by Cyril Connolly, is a book that mattered greatly to me when I was young. It does so, still. As a record of the risks that any gifted child confronts when trying to "deliver" on promise, it stays germane, though the terms of the problem have changed. Connolly writes of the difficulties posed by too great or small an intelligence, too indolent or active a nature, too elaborate or scant an education. He lists the "enemies" that await the artist of substantial or small physical beauty, considerable or insufficient wealth, sizable or no renown, an absence or overlarge dose of ambition, and so on. His tale remains, I think, a cautionary one. As he puts it, "The best thing that can happen for a writer is to be taken up very late or very early, when either old enough to take its measure, or so young that when dropped by society he has all life before him." That particular wunderkind squandered his gifts, or at least did not deploy them in the fashion he had planned. His single published novel, *The Rock Pool,* is a work far less enduring and engaging than the autobiographical *Enemies of Promise* or his meditative *The Unquiet Grave.* He's now remembered, if at all, as a critic and an editor rather more than as a creative writer; the dream of a great fiction stayed unrealized at Connolly's death. But his prescient listing of the "enemies" of talent ought to be required reading; it holds just as current today.

Yet one of the things that feel different, at the present moment, than was the case when I began — not to mention in Connolly's time — is the prospect of an extended career. It was standard in "the good old days" but now seems comparatively rare. A gallery would sponsor a young painter in the hope that his or her third exhibition might make money. An editor would take on a writer in the hope that the fourth or fifth book would yield a profit; in the contemporary marketplace a second book is harder to sell— unless its predecessor was a commercial success—than a first. In an age of computerized tracking of sales and website "hits," there's a concomitant risk of failure and ensuing disappointment. The old instruction "If at first you don't succeed, then try and try again" is harder to put into practice; there are fewer chances for a second act.

In every career and context the opening gambit seems both brave and tentative: a first move, then a second, then a third. And, as in any game of chess, there's an opening, a middle game, and an end. Let us focus on that opening game: the first moves.

The first moves in a game of chess are formulaic, largely: a se-ries of preliminary gambits that configure what's to come. It's the "Queen's Gambit" or "King's Indian" or "Ruy Lopez" or some other opening sequence that takes relatively little thought, having been established over time. Even the prodigious child will be, to start with, formulaic; there are a finite number of ways to begin a contest, and only after its first sequence will the shape of the game declare itself and strategies unfold. The pattern is predict-able—or changed at risk—until the pieces are "developed," a quasi-technical term in chess, and the "attack" proper begins.

Bobby Fischer became an International Grand Master at four-teen, and World Chess Champion fourteen years thereafter. An article in the *New York Times* announces that a nine-year-old from

California has become the youngest U.S. Chess Master (a lower ranking than International Grand Master, but possibly an augury). Samuel Sevian "set the record on Dec. 11 [2010], at the age of 9 years, 11 months and 11 days by tying for first in a small tournament at the Mechanics Institute in San Francisco. He broke the record held by Nicholas Nip, a San Francisco resident, by 11 days." There's something a touch Guinness-bookish about such record keeping, but mastery in one so young is worth reporting on.

For years I myself was enthralled by the game, playing long hours with my parents and my elder brother. Once I beat my brother, who just had drawn a match with someone who once drew with someone who once drew with someone who once beat Capablanca (1888–1942), the great Cuban-born world champion. By my childhood logic, that made *me* chess champion of the world. In actuality I was a good bad player, at best a bad good player, and would fall asleep at night while calculating combinations and adjusting a response. I never advanced beyond a middling competence, but the game still seems to me a kind of paradigm for mental agility — the ability to see two, three, five, then seven moves ahead.

There has long been an anecdotal linkage between mathematics and music, and the two forms of composition do seem somehow akin; it's not a one-to-one equivalence, but the young performer in one field may well have a taste for the other. And I wonder if silence (a strict convention in chess tournaments) isn't somehow a contributing factor in these endeavors also; the buzz we've grown so used to in our modern world was not omnipresent in the lifetimes of Newton or Bach. When Antonio Stradivari built his stringed instruments in seventeenth-century Cremona, he had no need to contend with the roar of automobile and air-plane, not to mention boom box and washing machine; the hum we take for granted now—in computers, furnaces, fluorescent lights—was less a factor then.

*Silence.* Is it sentimental to suggest that the rapt attention chil-dren pay to page or drawing pad or keyboard constitutes a marker for young talent? We worry nowadays about multitasking, the in-cessant bleep of BlackBerry and iPod; attention deficit hyperac-tivity disorder and autism seem somehow two sides of the same coin, two ways of living in the world amid a welter of distraction. I don't of course mean that these diseases are engendered by the clatter of modernity, or that their epidemic proportions could be reduced by fewer stimuli. Nor do I mean that ADHD and autism might be strategies concocted by the body to deal with the assault of cell phone, Twitter, and computer games. But the idiot savant may well be a subset of the category "prodigy"—the mathemati-cal whiz who forgets to tie his or her own shoelaces; the calen-drical pedant who knows if August 27, 1787, was a Tuesday or a Thursday, but not the present weather or the time of day. Con-centrated focus has much to do with creative achievement; it can't be managed with one hand or only intermittent attention. The mind must not wander or drift.

This is debatable. Problems get solved while we sleep. It's pos-sible to argue that precisely such "wander or drift" is what her-alds the conceptual breakthrough and a mind at fruitful work. The sidelong glance and directionless ramble may well be an important part of the creative process. But I'm not talking about accidental-seeming inspiration or the sudden perception of order in what once appeared chaotic. These require deep immersion; the *eureka* moment in a bathtub comes only to those who, consciously or no, are grappling with a problem while they soak.

So the child who's left alone to play is also doing work. To make of transience permanence: such is the high charge of art. Often it's an idle or a casual enterprise: a set of scribbles on the page or a whistled tune. Sometimes this comes from parental instruction, the lessons learned at an elder's knee and during odd hours at home. Sometimes it grows out of more formal study: the expectation of a doting or strict teacher that Dick or Jane will learn. And once it's clear that Dick or Jane is gifted, a schedule gets arranged or rearranged accordingly. The ballerina's mother and the father who's a tennis coach clear the decks for practice, insisting on long hours spent at the barre or net. The virtuoso or the prodigy is shielded from such matters as grocery shopping and laundry, the *busy*-ness of life.

What strikes me now when I think back on youth is the untrammeled time available for play each day—to paint or read or run through scales—and how adult worldly matters, "getting and spending," didn't enter in. There were no bills to pay or calls to make or taxes to prepare; there were no errands to run or emails and text messages to answer. There were fewer distractions, perhaps, fewer temptations to avoid or meetings to attend; there were no rooms to clean and lawns to mow. (Or, more precisely, the meetings and the rooms and lawns were not my proper business; it only recently came clear to me that other folk were hard at work enabling my own indolence.) So it's silence I remember, the privacy and inward-facing space. I was precocious, not prodigious, but the time to dream away the day was time, I'm sure, well spent.

Sex enters into "the art of youth" also, and almost from the start. The desire to be noticed and hunger for approval are aspects of early performance that should not be underestimated, a kind of quasi-erotic appetite for fame. The need to make an impression on a piece of paper or a canvas is not, perhaps, in essence distinct from the wish to impress an acquaintance or attractive stranger; it's making one's mark in the private, then public arena. "Ratification" and "gratification" are adjacent terms. I can't remember when I first understood that words could be romantic, and a girl would like you better if you sent her a poem on Valentine's Day. Or, later, when I recognized that being a writer was likely to get you a lady's attention and, later still, a bed. For musicians and painters this holds just as true; there's an act of self-assertion, a reaching out to others that may prove seductive. "To score" or "to make," in the slang of our adolescence, meant "to have sex with" as well as "to compose" or "to produce." The painter and his model are a standard image of "coupling," as are the poet and muse. As the old limerick puts it:

> While Titian was mixing rose madder,
> His model posed nude on a ladder.
> Her position, to Titian,
> Suggested coition.
> So he climbed up the ladder and had her.

In chess, the middle game is where strategy takes precedence: strength builds or is depleted; the lines of play grow clear. The complicating imperatives of defense and attack enter in. A musician or writer or painter who has established a position after an opening series of moves must decide, as does a chess player, which lines to pursue, which to abandon. Such terms as "development" and "sacrifice" become germane; the contestant or artist at this stage must deal with and confront an often-bewildering array of possibilities. Each choice is consequential, even crucial, to success. And such decisions ramify; the game takes its shape early on.

Consider, once again, the three brief lives here described. "The Open Boat" seems emblematic of the career of its author — an adventure, then explosion, a small craft set adrift on troubled seas. Much was heroically salvaged, much lost. The career of Carrington began with éclat and ended in near paralysis; those who applauded her at the Slade School were no doubt disappointed by the self-effacement of her later years. But the art she left behind has an integrity and seriousness that continue to reward attention; long after death, her reputation grows. The composer's career was not the same; "the art of youth," for Gershwin, enlarged into full-throated song, and he was at or near the height of productive achievement at life's close.

A youthful death, in these three instances, made for three very different finales. Only the suicide has a self-imposed conclusiveness; the two men lost to illness would have kept on keeping on. And it's impossible to say with certainty what their middle game and endgame would have looked like — or, rather, these were incorporate in the opening moves. The towheaded boy (who walked into the water while his brothers watched) and the immigrants' child (who played the piano the day it arrived through the window) both offer up self-portraits as a kind of time-lapse exposure: beginnings conjoined to their ends.

My first novel—the one I began for John Updike—was published in 1966; I was twenty-three. *The Martlet's Tale* proved, it's fair and not boastful to say, a success; the reviews were generous; my photograph was widely reproduced in newspapers and magazines; four years later a movie was made. In 1966 as well I was hired by Bennington College to replace the eminent author Bernard Malamud, who planned to take a leave of absence from the faculty. I was, in short, one of those fortunate children whom American elders anoint and appoint; all systems did seem "go."

In retrospect it seems to me the middle game was entered then; there were other lines of play. My contemporaries did not have, I think, the anxiety about employment that obtains today; we simply assumed we'd find jobs. In terms of earning a living, for instance, I might have found myself welcome in some part of the industries of publishing or entertainment. I'd spent a brief period in London, working for my uncle in his art gallery (Roland, Browse & Delbanco) on Cork Street; I toyed too with the idea of diplomacy and the foreign service. But by choosing to teach in the hills of Vermont, I took a decision—half-conscious at best— to turn my back on those other careers and to embrace the role of author-teacher. I told myself it would last for a season and then I'd resume my "public" life, go back to Manhattan and the fast track on which I had started to run. Instead, I fell under the spell of New England and the privacy of writing books; the world of public commerce was a world I left behind.

All this took place not merely decades but a century, a millennium ago. My next two novels, *Grasse, 3/23/66* (1968) and *Consider Sappho Burning* (1969), were so resolutely experimental that, by the 1970s, I was no longer a potential best seller but a novelist more recognized than read. I'm reporting on all this in shorthand since the present point is not my own publishing history but the way a road not taken has as many turns and byways as the one we tread.

One further set of similes will bring this to a close. A career in art is like a chess game, possibly; it is also a contest of speed. "Slow but steady wins the race" is the moral of the fable of the tortoise and the hare. But Aesop must have been imagining a marathon, or at least substantial distance; "slow but steady" would not win the hundred-yard dash. Therefore it depends upon what kind of race is being described; the steady forward motion of the cross-country walker will allow for large stretches traversed but not at a sprinter's pace. And insofar as the art of youth is a hundred-yard dash, not a marathon, the skills of acceleration and a rapid stride pertain.

So the young athlete or artist bursts out of the starting blocks—arms flailing, legs pumping like pistons, eyes staring straight ahead. Her wind is good, his spirits high; the race seems fun to run. A first publication or gallery show or performance of a symphony has been well received, much applauded, and she qualifies for this event. It is "invitation only," and his name has been selected; hard training has ensued. The lanes in the track are defined. There are other athletes, all running as well, some at the same rate, some faster, some slower: a bunched pack at the first turn. They see their friends, their lovers, and their adversaries running; they redouble their efforts, lap after lap, and catch or do not catch a second wind.

End of comparison. What Updike called "the little ecstasy of extracting resemblances from different things" can carry us only so far. The metaphor seems apt enough — for there's an element of physicality in most efforts of the youthful artist — but the work of a poet or painter is only tangentially akin to that of the hurdler or sprinter. In these brief paragraphs I've used the analogies of chess and track and field; it's time now to shed metaphor and report on what took place.

"The hospital of Rhodes squats on the hill that rises to be Monte Smith." This is the first sentence of my first novel, *The Martlet's Tale,* and I wrote it again and again till satisfied; whatever its merits or failings it's a line on which I worked hard. Then there came the next line, then the next. I can remember sitting — those were the days of the portable typewriter — at a lamp-lit table in the predawn dark, or with my Smith Corona on my lap, on the east-facing stoop of a hut on Martha's Vineyard, with the sun rising in the early morning, or on a warm and bright midafternoon, and focusing, or trying to, on my self-imposed allotment of five hundred words a day. I had no telephone or television set; this was long before the era of the cell phone or computer; the silence would be broken only by a distant car or dog or gull or gust of wind. I'd read that Thomas Mann and Anthony Trollope had the daily expectation of a certain number of words composed; theirs seemed like models to follow and a good habit to have. Now with the advantage of hindsight it's clear I was establishing what would become a lifelong routine. I did not attend a writing conference or earn an MFA degree, less widespread then as initiation rites for the professional writer than is the case today. But all young artists must, I think, acquire their own systematic procedure; this was when and where I found mine.

My daily employment was in a fish market — Poole's Fish Market in Menemsha — where I'd report at 8 a.m. to load the fish truck with swordfish and crates of lobsters for delivery "down island" to the Woods Hole Ferry or to restaurants in Vineyard Haven, Edgartown, Oak Bluffs. The easy banter of the fisherman seemed like a language to learn. I reveled in the job, the reek of fish, my calf-high rubber boots, the bushels of quahogs and cherrystone clams. Taking the back roads of the island, wearing a green shirt with the logo *Poole's* stitched across its pocket, driving with the windows down to savor the inrushing mixture of air — pine needles and sea wrack and wood smoke — shifting gears and singing loudly to myself, off-key, I felt both a part of the workforce and a word serf set free from the desk.

My boss was a gruff New Englander whose father and grandfather had been fishermen, as would be his own son in turn; my summertime coworkers were the children of the privileged, and all of us felt lucky to earn Everett Poole's derision: "You call that a *fillet?* You call that floor *clean?*" With his three stooges — me and the sons of the dean of NYU and the president of Yale — he was stern and impatient and fine. He'd calculated, or so I assume, that our presence behind the counter would bring in friends or relatives as customers — the moneyed folk of Martha's Vineyard who found our presence charming and stopped by to say hello. Each morning he berated us, chomping on an unlit cigar, telling us to lift the swordfish higher as we raised it to the pickup's bed, to wipe down our filleting knives more carefully, to cut closer to the bone. He worked harder and much more efficiently than any of those he employed. His brusque bluster too was picturesque, an island "character" who took no guff from millionaires or cabinet members and stars.

I myself was paid next to nothing in cash, though I could take home dead one-clawed lobsters or littlenecks whose shells were badly cracked. At ten minutes to eight each morning I drove to the dock in my Alfa Romeo convertible, then traded it for the broken-down Dodge delivery truck, with its loose clutch and battered tailgate, feeling as happy behind the one wheel as the other. I did this for four years—working from Memorial to Labor Day, six mornings a week. Sometimes I accomplished my language quota before "duty" kicked in; more often I returned to the windswept hill in Chilmark at noon (my days were half-days only) and wrote till the limit was reached. Then it was time to go out in the world—to go for a swim or a walk on the beach, to take my kayak to a pond or attend a party. In this fashion I was introduced to many of the "local" writers—Art Buchwald, Max Eastman, Leon Edel, Shirley Ann Grau, Lillian Hellman, John Hersey, Felicia Lamport, Joseph Lash, William Styron, and others. Saul Bellow, Bernard Malamud, Philip Roth, and John Updike passed through. They made me welcome at picnics, games of Scrabble, Anagrams, the ceremony of drinks . . .

Then, one morning in late August 1966, with *The Martlet's Tale* just published and my job starting soon at Bennington College, I was carrying a crate of lobsters down the street in Edgartown. A girl in tennis whites approached me, gushing, "Aren't you Nicholas Delbanco?"

"Yeah, sweetie, what's it to you," I said, sweating, relighting my pipe.

"Well, I'll be in your class this September," she said, and I remember thinking I looked distinctly unprofessorial. Buttoning my shirt, I said, "That's nice, my dear, and what might your name be?" and knew my days in the fish market would be, thereafter, numbered.

What has continued to accrete is language: five hundred words a day. The third page of *The Martlet's Tale* begins: "She was old, Orsetta Procopirios." This was the name of the grandmother whose buried treasure powered the plot of the novel, and for weeks I dithered over the line's proper formulation: "Orsetta Procopirios was old" would have made more sense. But I told myself — and nearly half a century later can remember making the decision — that the first of these two versions sounded somehow like a translation from the Greek, and at any rate more quirky and inflected. For "inflected," today I'd substitute "affected," and would change the line to standard English — but all such water's long under the bridge. Like any other author I would write a phrase over and over, playing with the rhythm and the sequence of the syllables, convincing myself that an "and" or an "or" was crucial to the line's success, declaiming my prose to the echoing air and arranging the shape of the sound.

Apprenticeship has many guises; I served mine out on a hilltop off the coast of Massachusetts in the mid-1960s. I know, of course, how fortunate I was to start to write seriously there and then — how well heeled was my poverty, how happily abjured my celibacy, how intermittent my silence and focused my devotion. Born Vineyarders would say that they were "going to America" when they took the ferry off-island. I myself left long ago and have returned only rarely; I married a girl from America whose allegiance is to Cape Cod. I open littlenecks and oysters now with a less practiced wrist; I've not seen or eaten—much less delivered—a hand-harpooned swordfish in years. I no longer teach at Bennington or call New England home. Much changes and has changed. But the labor of writing a sentence, rewriting it, *rewriting* it is still a labor I love.

# Conclusion

I am not young enough to know everything.

— OSCAR WILDE

"NEL MEZZO DEL CAMMIN DI NOSTRA VITA." So begins
the epic journey of *La Divina Commedia*, when its author, Dante
Alighieri, is thirty-five years old; he here divides the Biblical expectation of a lifetime into halves. This was more a symbolic than
statistically accurate junction; in 1300, few wayfarers at thirty-five
could have been described as at "the middle of the road of our
life." The author-pilgrim finds himself (*"mi ritrovai per una selva
oscura"*) in an "obscure" or dark wood, *"ché la diritta via era smarrita."* *"Smarrita"* is the word of the first stanza most susceptible to
various translations; Dante has been walking on a path in a forest,
and all directions seem "tangled" or "blocked" or "confused." He
must decide how to continue, and which way to proceed.

By the twentieth century, however, a life span of seventy was
not too much to expect. Whereas Dante wrote in exile from his
beloved Florence, the poet Robert Frost spent the bulk of his time

close to home. The New England he wrote of was familiar, not imagined or remembered; he spent years as a not-so-gentlemanly farmer trying to wrest profit from the land. What Dante called *"la diritta via"* — "the straight way" — was, for Frost, a well-worn path. Nonetheless, he too would contemplate alternatives in "The Road Not Taken." "Two roads diverged," Frost writes, and "I, I took the one less traveled by," which, by his own accounting, "made all the difference." That moment when we pause and choose which direction to take next is the moment when first acts conclude.

This predicates, of course, the notion of a second act: a branching road and an additional path available to follow. Both Dante and Frost lived long; the great Italian poet's dates were 1265 to 1321, the American's were 1874 to 1963. The former's dates are inexact, since we're not wholly sure of the year of his birth, but to have died at fifty-six in the early fourteenth century is to have earned the assertion that one travels far (from *Inferno* to *Paradiso*). And Robert Frost became the very emblem of a white-haired sage; his recital of "The Gift Outright" at John F. Kennedy's Presidential Inauguration, on January 20, 1961, is part of our national album: old age conferring blessings upon a chosen youth.

But true first acts have no sequel. At the risk of being arithmetically overcute, the average age of our three figures at death was thirty-five; collectively they lived 104 years, and had Carrington committed suicide just three weeks later, the sum would reach 105. What Dante cited as the middle of his journey's road, and where he commenced his epic, is for our trio a completion: *Finita la Commedia*. We leave them at a junction point, a literal dead end.

I have not written earlier of the sorrow attaching to rapid

success since its overarching affect has to do with pleasure. But there's a way that great good luck can come to seem an albatross around the neck of him or her who has it; not least, perhaps, comes the question of if and in what fashion that good luck was earned. There follows as well the perpetual question *what next?* To consider one's position in a race too curiously is to risk one's place at the head of the pack. The runner stumbles while watching her feet; a hitter's swing can lose its rhythm when too closely watched. That backward look by which triumphant Orpheus turned the recovery of his beloved Eurydice into failure, hard on the heels of his great expedition, is a cautionary tale for all who pay a visit to the Underworld; best to forge blindly ahead.

Of the three artists I here profile, Carrington was the most self-conscious, most continually aware of the difficulties involved in her creative endeavor. It's not an accident that her output was, by comparison with Crane's and Gershwin's, much the most constrained. For her, as I suggested, the best became the enemy of the merely better, and her self-censoring grew harsher even as she grew more expert in her craft. The other two enjoyed an unconstrained inventiveness that seems a component of "the art of youth." These creative personalities were fluent almost to the point of excess, and in Crane's case a deal of chaff surrounded the kernels of grain. Neither the writer nor the composer was given to self-doubt, though sometimes to self-deprecation, and their expressive urgency did not admit of obstacles; they wrote and wrote and wrote.

So at what point, if any, did they query their good fortune; when, if ever, did they fear the curtain was going to fall? With Carrington, it seems, such fear was a constant companion; to Gershwin it was a stranger, for Crane a sometime-visitor he hosted at the end. There's a distinction too between the ruddy health of Carrington—it feels as though she would have lived long if left to her natural life span—and that of the feverish Crane. Here it's Gershwin who splits the difference; he seemed in excellent health and physical condition until the tumor grew.

Where they went, they traveled quickly: no half measures or thwarted experience here. Gershwin, Crane, and Carrington had in common curtailed lives that were nonetheless full. And they were always at work. The first was almost constantly composing or performing, the second at his desk or bent across his notebook; the third took down her pictures from the wall. One died in straitened circumstance; one killed herself; one was attended fruitlessly by a team of doctors. In Badenweiler a lone woman kept vigil; in Ham Spray there were servants; in Hollywood when Gershwin died a national mourning ensued. As I suggested early on, while trying to describe the contours of *The Art of Youth,* together these three seem to me to cover the terrain.

Near the end of such diverging roads, I want to take one further path and offer a digression about the writing life—and how, for this particular author, it took shape and form.

My parents both were refugees from Hitler's Germany. Separately, they fled to London, where they met again and were married; in the late 1940s, with two young sons in tow, they settled in a suburb of New York. My early memories are of a gathering of exiles: chamber music, schnapps, the smell of roses and Chanel No. 5, the sound of heels and wooden canes on polished parquet floors.

Visitors would share their stories: whose relatives were lost or had survived, who prospered or was failing, and who needed help.

One such couple, I remember, had a romantic story; they had escaped from Paris on a pair of homemade bicycles hours before Nazis seized the city. The man—like my father—had been born in Hamburg, and he was good at drawing and had a childlike eye. His name was Hans Augusto Reyersbach, her name was Margret, and they had written books about Pretzel the Dog and Rafi the Giraffe. Neither of these publishing ventures was particularly successful, and they came, by way of South America, to the United States. The couple next collaborated on a book about an inquisitive monkey and called it *Curious George.* By the time they came to see us, the Reys (like the Gershwins, they had changed their name) were famous and well off. I remember my mother served more than usually abundant pastries, and that she used the good china and told me to wear a clean shirt.

Mr. Rey was plump, in a brown suit, and he wore glasses and was balding and round-faced and kind. He had a manner with children both easy and unforced. He knew about the stars and, in 1952, would publish a book about them; on a previous visit he had taken me into the garden and shown me constellations in a way that made me *see.* We were sitting in the living room, and he stood off to one side. Suddenly, I heard, "Nicky, help! It's Curious George and I'm stuck in the fireplace and can't move. Come help me, won't you please?"

I looked around. Mrs. Rey, unconcerned, drank her tea. But Mr. Rey, upright by the piano, had a strained expression on his face; his Adam's apple bobbed up and down, and his lips twitched soundlessly. "Tommy!"—now it was my brother's turn to be addressed—"It's the Man in the Yellow Hat, and I'm looking for Curious George and can't find him anywhere. Where do you think he might be?"

This went on for some time. Turn by turn we were cajoled by creatures from a storybook, and even then I knew enough to know I was supposed to act surprised. We boys jumped up and looked in the fireplace chimney; we tried to pretend the man in our living room—I had watched Edgar Bergen and Charlie Mc-Carthy and knew about ventriloquists—was *not* playing Curious George. He was very bad at it. He squeaked and perspired and moved his mouth and only when he said good-bye and wiped his face and shrugged himself into his overcoat did he seem an adult again. I remember thinking, as I watched them drive away in their fine clothes and gleaming car, well, a person can get rich by pretending to be someone else and then by throwing his voice.

*Voice.* I have been trying to throw it all my writing life. Ventriloquists are few and far between, and very few are good at it, and authors don't routinely work in distant vocal registers. Yet in some central way I date my love of the profession to the sight and sound of H. A. Rey being foolish in our living room—a Pied Piper in a tailored suit who, together with his artist-wife, constructed an enchantment for the young. Each time I light a fire now I think of that invented creature hidden in the chimney and ready to leap to the page.

*First acts.* Imagine a girl from the provincial town of Bedford hearing that she's just received the Slade School's first prize for Figure Painting and for Painting from the Cast. Imagine a piano-playing song-plugger learning that Al Jolson will record his composition and make it a surefire hit. Imagine a boy from New Jersey being praised by Hamlin Garland and publishing a novel at the age of twenty-one. The other two are not even that old, and they must have told themselves that theirs would be smooth sailing after such a start.

Creative work is largely done in private, even anonymity; its maker may well stay unsung. But "the art of youth" has been here defined as something someone notices, a public performance and hat in the ring. Crane, Carrington, and Gershwin earned favorable recognition from their elders as well as their peers; the men reaped commercial rewards. It's a heady brew, this sort of notice; it causes one to pinch oneself and straighten up and look around. What did they see, this trio of young artists; what sort of vista was opening out, and did they envision a sequel to their auspicious debuts?

I think so. I think they must have imagined picture after picture, book after book, and tune after tune. The sky's the limit for each Icarus until wings start to melt. As W. H. Auden writes in his great poem "Musée des Beaux Arts," "About suffering they were never wrong, the old Masters," and his image of a young man drowning off at the edge of Bruegel's picture does point to "its human position"—the tumble pride will take. That boy who plummets seaward while the world goes on about its business is a cautionary figure, legs unstrung. Yet for the bulk of their brief lives (and certainly in Gershwin's), there seemed no outer limit to what they would accomplish; as with Icarus, the trajectory they dreamed of was always, only up.

The falling off for Carrington was not so much a failure of

talent as of the conviction that art itself can matter. The falling off for Crane was a squandering of the belief that artistry must count. In Gershwin's case I think it more an issue of too much too soon and the burden of high expectation; he drove himself in too many directions for "the straight road" to be clear. Yet the collapse of all three figures is less instructive than the size of their prior achievement; their exits tell us less than do their entrances. If nothing else, these first acts leave one wondering what might have been accomplished in a third or fifth . . .

As Henry James observed of Crane, "I think of him with such a sense of possibilities & powers." Of Carrington it's safe to say that, had she continued to function as artist, she would have continued to grow; of Gershwin the same holds true. Regret must thereby enter in, if only because the art of youth is of necessity a passing thing. Although it need not always end, as William Wordsworth feared, in "despondency and madness," it does need to end. The saga of Sixto Rodriguez with which this book begins is an exception to the rule; the South Africans who found him after forty years of near-total obscurity were reversing what another William — Shakespeare — called "the whirligig of time." Sugar Man has the chance to revisit his past; Crane, Carrington, and Gershwin died too soon.

*The art of youth.* Although theirs are separate stories, certain shared motifs emerge: energy, a need to produce that borders on compulsion, a personal élan. Each of them was outward-facing as well as self-absorbed; each worked in various subsets of their chosen fields. Crane wrote poetry and journalism in addition to prose fiction; Carrington tried her hand at almost every aspect of the visual arts; Gershwin wrote and was planning to write in a number of musical modes. And I *do* think we can tell, with no carbon dating required, that all three of them—the author of *The Red Badge of Courage,* the painter of those fresh-faced girls, the composer of *Rhapsody in Blue*—were young. When Crane calls his protagonist "the youth," or Carrington paints market scenes, or Gershwin composes a dance ditty for a pair of lovers, there's something jaunty and hopeful about both maker and thing made. The rate of composition and the rush toward completion belong somehow to someone starting out.

Ambition has gradations, but they were each ambitious; success too has gradations and they were variously fortunate after their debuts. The men found fame, the woman not, but all three were applauded from the start. The least they did was more than most, their best as good as anything the period can claim. In this context, plausibly, what we deal with is a natural life span writ small and not large, *vivace* and not *lento.* Since the desired end point is the same—a masterpiece—the creative artist whose sojourn is brief must work at a more rapid pace. Our trio did pass through the stages of age, yet they did so much more urgently than those whose time encompasses a fifth or ninth decade.

Crane, Carrington, and Gershwin were seriously playful and, at times, extravagant; these people had a way of being noticed in a room. Worldly yet ethereal, they were—by widespread attestation—an excitement to know. Our artists shared a grave exuberance, a conviction that this life can be expressed in and celebrated by music, art, and literature, and that it need not end. "Art is long and life is brief," perhaps, but when "the art of youth" transacts its blithe transformational magic, both art and life are both.

# *Author's Note*

Since this is less a work of scholarship than speculative inquiry, I have not appended the full apparatus of research: footnotes, an index, a bibliography. I have consulted dozens of books, and most are referenced here below, but the principal source matter for these pages is the creative labor of my subjects: their writing, their painting, their music. In the biography-based chapters of the text—Chapters 2 through 4—I have relied on prior documentation as well as the expertise of predecessors; to the best of my knowledge the citations that follow are accurate. But these notes are in summary mode rather than exhaustive, and I can only hope they lead the reader to additional study on and of their own.

# *Notes*

### Introduction

The definition of "prodigy" comes from the *Oxford English Dictionary*, vol. 8 (Oxford: Oxford University Press, 1961), pp. 1420–1421.

### 1. First Acts

Much of this information—on the ages of poets, musicians, and kings—is culled from *The Book of Ages: Who Did What When?* by Desmond Morris (New York: Penguin Books, 1985).

### 2. Stephen Crane

The first description of Crane's lineage ("A Crane had sailed with Sir Francis Drake . . .") comes from *The Portable Stephen Crane*, ed. Joseph Katz (New York: Viking Press, 1969), p. vii. Much of the data and recollections that follow can be found in *The Crane Log: A Documentary Life of Stephen Crane, 1871–1900*, eds. Stanley Wertheim and Paul Sorrentino (New York: G. K. Hall & Co., 1994), and the two-volume *The Correspondence of Stephen Crane*, eds. Wertheim and Sorrentino (New York: Columbia University Press, 1988). The first quotation ("This morning at 5:30 . . .") comes from *The Crane*

*Log,* pp. 2–3, as does the recollection "Notes on the life of Stephen Crane by his Brother, Edmund B. Crane," p. 10. Additional citations from *The Crane Log* include McClurg's attack on "The Red Badge of Hysteria," p. 179; the inscription to Frank Harris, p. 269; and the argument from the "General Editor's Preface," by Philip Holthaus, that "early fame . . . did . . . more harm than good," p. ix. Further quotations from *The Crane Log* include the letters to Lily Brandon Munroe and Nellie Crouse, and the dedication to "C.E.S." on pp. 95, 175, and 226 respectively. That text is also the source for Cora's lament "My letters are one long inky howl," p. 353, and Willa Cather's memorial tribute, p. 126.

The assertion that Stephen was "a good and quiet baby" comes from his first biography, *Stephen Crane: A Study in American Letters,* by Thomas Beer, with an introduction by Joseph Conrad (New York: Alfred A. Knopf, 1926), pp. 35–36. So do the recollection of playing baseball at Claverack College, p. 53, and the dismissal of Émile Zola's *La Débâcle,* pp. 97–98. The recollections of his colleague by Joseph Conrad come from his introduction to that volume. Ford Madox Ford's descriptions of Crane's character and the landscape of Brede Place can be found in his *Return to Yesterday* (New York: H. Liveright & Co., 1932), pp. 36–37. In the same vein, H. G. Wells writes of the "the marvelous Christmas party" in his *Experiment in Autobiography* (New York: Macmillan Co., 1934), pp. 522–523. Henry James's condolence letter to Cora is included in *The Letters of Henry James,* vol. 1, ed. Percy Lubbock (New York: Charles Scribner's Sons, 1920), p. 315. As to the question of the difficulty Crane presents his biographers: Thomas Beer's book, though incisive, is full of factual error and invented detail; John Berryman's biography is penetrating but loosely speculative; R.

W. Stallman's is studious but overreliant on Beer. The most judicious of them, it seems to me, is Christopher Benfey's *The Double Life of Stephen Crane* (New York: Alfred A. Knopf, Inc., 1992), and its very title signals the problem of how to describe this complicated man.

The principal repository of Crane's correspondence resides in the two-volume edition (eds. Wertheim and Sorrentino) from which I quote the letter about his ancestor "captured by some Hessians," vol. 1, p. 166, and the letters about studying at Syracuse and the pleasures of a saddle horse, pp. 63 and 166–167 respectively. The *Correspondence* is also the source for the letter claiming to be "often dishonest" and the one to his editor Ripley Hitchcock, vol. 1, pp. 209 and 213 respectively. "I have heard a great deal about genius lately . . ." comes from pp. 230–231 of the same volume, as does the letter "So you lack females of the white persuasion . . . ," p. 44. Cora's letter to Arnold Bennett comes from the *Correspondence*, vol. 2, p. 682, and Stephen's letter warning an unnamed correspondent not to talk about his health in front of Mrs. Crane is on p. 504. The letter from Robert Barr to Karl Harriman comes from *Stephen Crane: Letters*, eds. R. W. Stallman and Lillian Gilkes (New York: New York University Press, 1960), p. 287. *The Complete Poems of Stephen Crane*, edited and with an introduction by Joseph Katz (Ithaca, New York: Cornell University Press, 1993), is the source for the poems that begin "A man said to the universe," "My cross!," and "Many red devils ran from my heart," as well as the chapter's epigraph. The authoritative edition of Crane's work is the ten-volume *The Works of Stephen Crane*, ed. Fredson Bowers (Charlottesville: University Press of Virginia, 1969–1976), and all the quotations from his prose can be found therein. But, for example, to cite the passage from the short story "The Veteran" ("When the roof fell in . . .") as coming from *The Works of Stephen Crane,* ed. Fredson Bowers, vol. 6 (Charlottesville: University Press of Virginia, 1971), p. 86, seems to me to be — given the nature of this overview — needlessly detailed. I have also consulted *Stephen Crane's Literary Family: A Garland of Writings,* ed. Thomas A. Gullason (Syracuse: Syracuse University Press, 2002) for the data on the Crane family, pp. 1–2, and the guidebook description of Brede Place by Augustus J. C. Hare in *Sussex* (London: George Allen, 1894), pp. 47–48. Hamlin Garland's inscribed copy of *Maggie: A Girl of the Streets* (1893) resides in the Lilly Library of Indiana University.

### 3. Dora Carrington

The first reference here, John Rothenstein's encomium, comes from his foreword to *Carrington: Paintings, Drawings, and Decorations,* by Noel Carrington (New York: Thames and Hudson, 1980), p. 13, and his comment that "she had another advantage, precocity" comes from the same text, p. 11. Noel Carrington, her brother, describes their shared history ("Dora Carrington, fourth child in a family of five . . .") in that text on p. 15, and his remark "At no stage of her family life . . ." comes from the same source. Further, he quotes Sacheverell Sitwell's guarded appreciation of his sister, p. 48. Michael Holroyd wrote the foreword to Jane Hill's *The Art of Dora Carrington* (New York: Thames and Hudson, 1994), and his comment about her "ghostlike and half-concealed . . . figure" can be found there on p. 7. Holroyd's fuller description of Carrington comes from his *Lytton Strachey: A Critical Biography* (New York: Holt, Rinehart and Winston, 1968), vol. 2, p. 161. Jane Hill

is the source for "Carrington cropped her 'mother's glory' . . . ,"
p. 11, and "Carrington loved Lytton more than ever . . . ," p. 64,
as well as the observation "Gerald has reserved his *'summa in-spiratio'* . . . ," p. 89. As of this writing, the books by her brother
and Ms. Hill contain the principal record of Carrington's life
and work, together with one full-length biographical study by
Gretchen Holbrook Gerzina, *Carrington: A Life* (New York: W. W.
Norton & Co., 1989). This last is the source for the quotations
from *D.C. Partridge, Her Book,* Carrington's diary now in the British Library. These entries ("Happiness in life . . . ," p. 283; "a sort
of overboiling seizes me . . . ," p. 280; and Lytton's "Remember,
all the bird books . . . ," p. 285) can be found in Gerzina; the last is
dated March 20, 1931.

The poem that begins "If my love were not impassioned . . ." is
cited in John Woodeson's *Mark Gertler: Biography of a Painter* (London: Sidgwick & Jackson, 1972), p. 232, and the exchange of letters
between Gertler and Carrington comes from the same source, pp.
241–247. Noel Carrington has edited *Mark Gertler: Selected Letters*
(London: Rupert Hart-Davis, 1965), and that text is the source of
Carrington's rueful "I loved my father . . . ," p. 144. Her lover Gerald Brenan wrote an autobiography, *A Life of One's Own* (London:
Jonathan Cape, 1962); on p. 236 he reports on Ralph Partridge's
letter about "a painting damsel . . ." Brenan's letter to V. S. Pritchett on April 4, 1979 ("my true medals") can be found in *Best of
Friends: The Brenan-Partridge Letters* (London: Chatto & Windus,
1986), p. 9. Leon Edel's collective biography of the central figures
in Bloomsbury is *Bloomsbury: A House of Lions* (New York: J. B.
Lippincott & Co., 1979), and his description of Carrington can be
found on p. 223.

Letters from Carrington as quoted by Jane Hill now reside in the Harry Ransom Humanities Research Center, the University of Texas at Austin (to Lytton Strachey), p. 26, and in the British Library (to Alix Strachey), p. 100. The vast majority of her letters and diary entries (to Strachey and Brenan, etc.) can be found in *Carrington: Letters and Extracts from Her Diaries,* ed. David Garnett (London: Jonathan Cape, 1970). As with the quotations from Stephen Crane's prose, it does not seem needful here to identify each of the letters and diary entries; to report that David Garnett's observations ("Like a child, she found it hateful to choose . . ." and "It did not occur to Lytton . . .") come from *Carrington: Letters and Extracts from Her Diaries,* ed. David Garnett (London: Jonathan Cape, 1970), pp. 12 and 13 respectively seems supernumerary now. The series of letters to Gerald Brenan from 1920 to 1932 can be located *seriatim* in that text. The temptation, indeed, is to quote unstintingly from her letters and her diaries; no better record of her personality exists.

### 4. George Gershwin

The quotation that ends with "bookmaking at Belmont Park" comes from *The Gershwins,* eds. Robert Kimball and Alfred Simon (Athenaeum: New York, 1973), p. xx. The next quotation ("a popular tune of the day") draws on that invaluable resource as well, p. xxii, as do the referents later in the chapter from Gershwin himself ("working at my compositions," p. 12) and the memorial recollections from Irving Caesar, Frances Gershwin, Kay Swift, and Edward G. Robinson (pp. 23, 47, 140, and 231 respectively). The chapter's final recollection (by Kitty Carlisle Hart) derives from the same source, p. 168. Another important compilation of memorabilia is Edward Jablonski's *Gershwin Remembered* (Portland, Oregon: Amadeus Press, 1992), from which I reproduce the quotations from Olin Downes, Virgil Thomson, Alexander Woollcott, S. N. Behrman, and Rouben Mamoulian, pp. 31, 124, 44, 66, and 70–71 respectively. Ira Gershwin's description of the arrival of a piano in the family home is reproduced in *George Gershwin,* ed. Merle Armitage (New York: Longmans, Green & Co., 1938; republished, with a new introduction by Edward Jablonski, in 1995), pp. 16–17. I also refer to *The George Gershwin Reader,* eds. Robert Wyatt and John Andrew Johnson (Oxford: Oxford University Press, 2004), for the quotations from Gershwin's own writings, "Our New National Anthem," "Fifty Years of American Music," and "The Composer in the Machine Age," pp. 91, 115, and 121 respectively.

The discussion of Izzy Baline and his incarnation as Irving Berlin comes from David Schiff's *Gershwin: Rhapsody in Blue* (Cambridge: Cambridge University Press, 1997), pp. 94–95, and the recollections of Charles Hambitzer derive from the same source, p. 16. That text has also provided me with the comment that Gershwin could be "selfish, narcissistic, emotionally stunted, occasionally cruel," p. 99, and the discourse on "modern music," written by Gershwin (November 1935), p. 18.

Howard Pollack's authoritative biography, *George Gershwin: His Life and Work* (Berkeley: University of California Press, 2006), is the source for the quotation on "critical approbation," p. 701, as well as the invitation by Paul Whiteman to compose what became *Rhapsody in Blue* ("an American Suite"), p. 296, and the recollection of the train trip Gershwin made to Boston ("actual substance"), p. 297. I also draw on Professor Pollack's comprehensive book for the list of instruments in *American in Paris,* p. 438, and the list of conductors who have performed the piece, p. 442. Gershwin's discussion of the difficulties of writing an opera is quoted by Pollack on pp. 463–64, and his description of Gershwin as a "champion shouter," as reported by Heyward, appears on p. 578. The funeral oration by Rabbi Wise is quoted by Pollack on pp. 214–215, and the tribute from Arnold Schoenberg on p. 134

Other sources include Charles Schwarz, *Gershwin: His Life and Music* (New York: Bobbs-Merrill Co., 1973) and David Ewen, *George Gershwin: His Journey to Greatness* (Upper Saddle River, New Jersey: Prentice-Hall, Inc., 1970). The composer's writings about his "own aspirations" are quoted from *George Gershwin,* ed. Larry Starr (New Haven: Yale University Press, 2011), p. 20, and Starr is also the source of the description of Gershwin "as the Brooklyn-born son of an immigrant Jewish couple from Russia . . . ," p. 3. The discussion of recruiting Todd Duncan comes from George Bornstein's *The Colors of Zion* (Cambridge: Harvard University Press, 2011), pp. 146–147, and Verna Arvey's recollection of Gershwin's desire to write about Lincoln is reported on by Walter Rimler, *George Gershwin: An Intimate Portrait* (Urbana: University of Illinois Press, 2009), p. 138

## 5. The Beginner
The referents to my own previously published work are to *Group Portrait: Conrad, Crane, Ford, James & Wells: A Biographical Study of Writers in Community* (New York: William Morrow, 1982), pp. 198–200, and *The Lost Suitcase: Reflections on the Literary Life* (New York: Columbia University Press, 2000), pp. 173–176. The quotation from Cyril Connolly's *Enemies of Promise* (Boston: Brown and Little,

1939) can be found on page 119 of that text, and the reference to "the little ecstasy" by John Updike comes from "Why I Write" in *Picked-Up Pieces* (New York: Alfred A. Knopf, 1975), p. 34. The title of U.S. Chess Master earned by Samuel Sevian at the record-setting age of nine was reported on in the *New York Times* National Edition, Sunday, December 12, 2010.

# Acknowledgments

Those who read all or part of this text include Alan Cheuse, Peter Ho Davies, Elizabeth Kostova, Daniel Okrent, Paul Theroux, Douglas Trevor, Robert Weisbuch, Stephen Whiting, and of course its dedicatee, my closest and final reader, Elena. I am deeply grateful and, as often before, in their debt. Rebecca Manery helped with the early stages of the research; Andrea Beauchamp helped, again, with her proofreader's eye and tracking down photographs; so too did Lynne Raughley. Robert Weisbuch walked with me through Evergreen Cemetery in Hillside, New Jersey. My agent, Gail Hochman of Brandt & Hochman, and my publisher, Laurence J. Kirshbaum, were, as always, indispensable from first to last; indeed, the shape of the whole was suggested by Larry at a breakfast meeting years ago—more years by now than either of us care to count. My newfound friends and colleagues Ed Park and Carmen Johnson of Amazon Books were unstinting in their practical support and critical acuity; Ed Park has proved himself an attentive editor indeed. Mary Beth Constant is, as a copyeditor, diligence itself. To each and all, my thanks.